Presented to

_____

From

_____

Date

_____

# Books by
# Vicki Caruana

FROM BETHANY HOUSE PUBLISHERS

---

*Apples of Gold for Teachers*

*One Heart at a Time*

VICKI CARUANA is foremost a teacher, speaking at educational and homeschool conferences nationwide. She is a frequent guest on various radio and television broadcasts, and her writing appears in many magazines. Vicki is the founder of Teachers in Prayer, and she lives in Colorado Springs, Colorado.

VICKI CARUANA

# ONE HEART at a TIME

## Inspirational Thoughts FOR TEACHERS

BETHANY HOUSE
Minneapolis, Minnesota

Published by Bethany House Publishers
11400 Hampshire Avenue South
Bloomington, Minnesota 55438

Bethany House Publishers is a division of
Baker Publishing Group, Grand Rapids, Michigan.

Printed in the United States of America

**Library of Congress Cataloging-in-Publication Data**

Caruana, Vicki.
  One heart at a time : inspirational thoughts for teachers / by Vicki Caruana.
    p.   cm.
  ISBN 0-7642-2793-9 (alk. paper)
  1. Christian teachers—Prayer-books and devotions—English.  I. Title.
  BV4596.T43C37    2004
  242'.68—dc22                                              2004012918

*Dedication*

EILEEN
LOVE YOU FOREVER

# Acknowledgments

To Julie Smith, my editor, fellow former teacher, and prayer warrior. Thank you for running with the vision of this book.

To the gang—Ellie, Steve, Christin, and Dave—
for holding me up in prayer as I wrote this book through
a difficult time in my life.

To Chip, Chris, Charles, Amy, Kevin, Matt, Kelly, Stan, Chad,
Jami, and Dad—you lift me up!

# Foreword

Some people tell me that as a high-school English teacher, I've got the toughest job in the world. I guess they're looking at the obvious—endless piles of essays to grade, a classroom full of hormones, nearly impossible state standards to reach, and a school budget that shrinks from year to year. As teachers we could get discouraged if we focused on the seemingly endless hurdles thrown in our path. Instead, I think we can choose to remember that we have been given a privilege as teachers: to change the world, *One Heart at a Time.*

That simple phrase is the positive focus of this wonderful new book by America's Teacher,™ Vicki Caruana, whose passion is to encourage teachers through her books and speaking. As I opened it on a Friday night after a long week of teaching and coaching, I found a friend—someone who has been in the classroom trenches, who understands our frustrations, and who knows how God's Word and helpful reminders can lift a tired spirit. When I closed it, I felt as though a fellow worker had bandaged my bruises, warmly hugged me, and filled me up with new resolve to continue pursuing my own calling to love and teach those teenagers the best way that I can.

If you want to change the world *One Heart at a Time*, I encourage you to open these pages to find just the refreshment you need to walk into your classroom each day.

## *Janet Holm McHenry*

Teacher, speaker, and author of
*Looking Up! Encouragement to Pursue a Life of Prayer*
*www.dailyprayerwalking.com*

# Contents

*Introduction* .......................... 11
1. Words Aptly Spoken .............. 13
2. Are You My Mother? ............. 17
3. Want to Leave a Legacy? .......... 21
4. First Timers ..................... 25
5. Expectations. .................... 28
*Weekend Words to Prepare Your Heart* .... 31
6. You Are Where You Belong ....... 32
7. Cover Your Bases ................ 36
8. Roll Call Prayer. .................. 40
9. Choose Mercy. ................... 44
10. Excess Baggage. .................. 48
*Weekend Words to Prepare Your Heart* .... 51
11. The Teachable Teacher ........... 53
12. Joy Stealers. ..................... 56
13. Veterans ........................ 59
14. Hopelessly Devoted. .............. 62
15. An Act to Follow ................ 65
*Weekend Words to Prepare Your Heart* .... 68
16. Cheerleader Barnabas ............ 70
17. A Workman Approved ............ 74
18. How Deep Is His Love? .......... 78
19. Called to Be Kind. ................ 82
20. Victory! ......................... 86
*Weekend Words to Prepare Your Heart* .... 89
21. The Liberty of Giving. ............ 91
22. Power Struggle ................... 95
23. I Don't Care Syndrome .......... 99
24. Enemy Mine ....................102

25. Like Manna From Heaven.........106
*Weekend Words to Prepare Your Heart*....110
26. When the Thrill Is Gone ..........111
27. Tender Mercies...................115
28. All for One and One for All .......118
29. Pursuit of Holiness ...............122
30. Copycat.........................126
*Weekend Words to Prepare Your Heart*....129
31. Pass It On.......................131
32. Who Is My Neighbor, Lord?.......134
33. True Hope......................138
34. Do As I Do .....................141
35. Truth Be Told...................145
*Weekend Words to Prepare Your Heart*....149
36. Sing From the Mountaintops......151
37. Name Above All Names...........155
38. Above and Beyond the Call of Duty ..158
39. Nothing Wasted .................161
40. Us Against Them ................164
*Weekend Words to Prepare Your Heart*....168
41. Those Who Rant and Rave ........170
42. The Bulletin Board of Faith .......173
43. Raise Your Hand ................177
44. Living a Life Worthy..............182
45. Put One Foot in Front of the Other ..185
*Weekend Words to Prepare Your Heart*....188
46. Great Is Your Faithfulness .........190
47. Milestone Markers ...............193
48. The King Is on His Throne........196
49. Gentlemen and Gentlewomen .....199
50. Open Classroom, Open Heart .....202
*Weekend Words to Prepare Your Heart*....205
Endnotes........................208

# Introduction

I*f only we could get into their hearts!* That's what I used to think would really make the difference with my students. What I realized is that getting into the heart is what makes the difference for all of us.

Education reform is only as effective as the teachers charged with its implementation. Unfortunately, many of us are already discouraged and brokenhearted over what our jobs have become. It is less about teaching and more about policy. But we can reach and teach our students if we first allow God to do a healing work in our own hearts.

Take time either before your day begins or at its end to meditate on God's truth, using the thoughts in this book. Over the next ten weeks, begin each school day with these thought-provoking meditations. Over the weekend, prepare your heart and mind with Weekend Words to Prepare Your Heart. Renewal happens step by step and one heart at a time. Let the Holy Spirit open the eyes of your heart so that you can then open the eyes of the hearts and minds of your students.

*Do not conform any longer to the pattern of this world, but be transformed by the renewing of your mind. Then you will be able to test and approve what God's will is—his good, pleasing and perfect will.* (Romans 12:2)

We can make a difference—*One Heart at a Time!*

*Vicki Caruana*
*www.applesandchalkdust.com*

Vicki with some of her first students—reaching and teaching one heart at a time! (Lockhart School, Tampa, Florida, 1985)

# I

# $\mathcal{W}$ORDS APTLY SPOKEN

## THE RIGHT WORDS

*The Lord God has given me his words of wisdom so that
I may know what I should say to all these weary ones.
Morning by morning he wakens me and opens my
understanding to his will.*

ISAIAH 50:4 TLB

## SPOKEN AT THE RIGHT TIME

This is a verse of expectancy! It is also one of submission.
It is so very important that we realize we are not the
authors of our expertise and abilities. God gives the words we
need. He is the one who makes His will clear to us. We can
expect that what He has called us to do He will also equip us
to do in His name.

The words we speak to those in our charge should not only be words of knowledge—an exhortation of facts and figures—but words of wisdom. These give life to those who are weary. The weary ones are those with troubled consciences or broken hearts. They need encouragement! They need God's words on the matter. And in order for us to be able to speak those words, we must first hear them for ourselves. "We must hear the word from God's mouth diligently and attentively, that we may speak it exactly."[1]

If we are to speak in a way that sustains the weary, we must do so with care, with sincere thought. We must measure our words so that we do not speak out of turn and cause hurt. We must balance our good intentions with proper preparation.

## BRING UNDERSTANDING AND PEACE

As a classroom teacher, parent-teacher conferences often unnerved me. Now as a parent, on the other side of the table, the familiar feeling deep in the pit of my stomach returns. That first conversation with a teacher is crucial. I want her to know that I understand the world in which she works. I want her to know that I support her efforts. But I also desperately want her to know and understand the needs of my child and to be willing to find ways to meet those needs.

We homeschooled our younger child for grades one through four. When he went back into public school in fifth grade, it was with trepidation—ours, not his! I prayed all summer about who God would choose for his teacher. I prayed for her and for myself, that I would be what she needed that year.

Good teachers know their subjects, such as reading, writing, math, science, and social studies. Great teachers know their subjects, too—our children! Mrs. Sanchez had my son pegged right away. She even went to the trouble of finding out each child's learning style, making them aware of it for themselves, and she used that knowledge to teach them more expertly. I was impressed from the very first day.

I met with Mrs. Sanchez often throughout the school year about how to help our son learn to do quality work and to stay motivated to do a good job. Our combined efforts produced a fifth-grade boy who understood the importance of hard work and appreciated the rewards that came with it. Because of Mrs. Sanchez I believe my son is ready to enter middle school. Without her words of wisdom and encouragement, I don't think he and I would have that confidence.

## ONE HEART AT A TIME

Words are powerful. Choose them carefully. Offer them
gently. Always use that power for good.

### PRAYER

*Heavenly Father, your words are truth! I know this
and treasure the fact. My words seem inadequate and
weak in comparison. My words spout my wisdom, and I
realize my wisdom is faulty. I want to be a life-giver to
my students. I want them to know you. Draw me to
yourself, and in the quiet places I will be a student of your
Word. Then and only then will I be able to offer the right
words at the right time to the right students. Thank you
for this opportunity to speak your words. Amen.*

# 2

# *A*RE YOU MY MOTHER?

## THE RIGHT WORDS

*We put no stumbling block in anyone's path, so that
our ministry will not be discredited.*

2 CORINTHIANS 6:3

## SPOKEN AT THE RIGHT TIME

The ultimate path we all walk is the one to God. God's Word illuminates the path, but there can be debris on the way that can make us falter and even fall. Sometimes there's enough in our way that we choose to leave the path marked out and go into the wilderness alone.

As teachers we are leaders in the lives of the families entrusted to us. For some, we may be the only ones who point out the path. Our leadership must be intentional not accidental. We must make the choice daily to lead with truth. If we focus on following the path ourselves, those who follow us will know the way as well. But if we ignore the influence our position holds in the lives of children, we are deceived and may become a stumbling block instead of one of God's lamps.

## BRING UNDERSTANDING AND PEACE

I watched this little girl wriggle herself away from her mother and run to my side. We had become close, this red-headed second grader and I. She was the daughter that I never had. But she belonged to someone else, and at that moment I felt like the bad guy.

Admittedly, her mom had some problems. Child services had been involved with this family more than once. Kids are good at giving second, and even more, chances, but something had happened that made this little one say, "Enough!"

"No, I don't want to go with you!" she shouted. "I want to stay with Miss Vicki."

The defeat I saw in that mother's eyes tore at my heart. She didn't fight back. She just slowly turned and walked out of my classroom.

No matter how much I felt for this child or how much I feel for all of my students, this felt wrong. Had I gotten in the way of their reconciliation? Had I broken up a family? All I wanted was to be a safe place for her. All I wanted was her best.

A mother's love is irreplaceable. A mother's love makes all the difference in this world. This mother loved her daughter. She wanted the best for her as well. My job was to be a bridge and not a wall.

I took this freckle-faced darling by the hand and walked her out to the parking lot. Her mother ran to meet us. In the moment of letting go, I didn't hand this precious one off to a mom who may or may not fail again. I gave her to a God who never fails. She will never be abandoned. She will always be sheltered under His wings. She will never be alone. She is right where she belongs.

## ONE HEART AT A TIME

Sometimes it's hard to see where our duty begins and ends when it comes to children. Basically our job is to connect children to God by way of our love for them. Be sure you are a help and never a hindrance.

## PRAYER

*Heavenly Father, I am humbled by the influence you have given me as teacher in the lives of these, your little ones. Help me to be mindful of this and to walk the path set before me with the intention of only following you!*

# 3
# $\mathcal{W}$ANT TO LEAVE A LEGACY?

## THE RIGHT WORDS

*Perseverance must finish its work so that you may be mature and complete, not lacking anything.*

JAMES 1:4

## SPOKEN AT THE RIGHT TIME

By God's grace alone we are kept alive. We receive all the virtue we need to do His work on earth and to make us fruitful. Most trees, when old, stop bearing fruit, but in God's trees the strength of grace does not fail even against the test of time and the elements. The latter days of a Christian's life are sometimes the best days, and the last work the best work: Perseverance is a sure evidence of maturity. God will make us complete and give us all we need in order to finally finish what is set before us.

## BRING UNDERSTANDING AND PEACE

The demands on a teacher are at times irrelevant and illogical. Teachers simply want to teach! We want to make a positive impact on the lives of children. It's a difficult thing to remember.

Kim Watson was new to our school, but not new to teaching. Married to a teacher-husband, she had all the support she needed at home. But at her new school that support wasn't enough. She had a vision for her students and wanted to leave them with something more than acceptable scores on the state test. Support for her vision ended the moment she entered the school each morning.

I watched as she implemented a new homework schedule, and parents balked. I watched as she raised her expectations, and her colleagues raised their eyebrows. I watched as she challenged the students with a new way to reach the state standards, and her principal raised her voice. Finally, when she asked for help on Fridays, I raised my hand. As a former teacher with a vision, I saw what Kim was trying to do—without support. As a parent of one of her students, I wanted to be that support she so desperately needed.

When the year was over and all was said and done, I asked

Kim how she thought the year went.

"Not nearly how I'd hoped," she confided. "I could have taken these kids so much farther!"

Her heart was broken. It's hard to do what you know you need to do to make a difference in the lives of children when your hands are tied or roadblocks are continually put in your way. Will she stay? Will she try again? I won't be there this time to help her. My child has moved on. I pray that God will provide just what she needs to do what she's been called to do.

## ONE HEART AT A TIME

We are proud of the fact that our students had high test scores, but our real hope is that we have made a difference that will carry students forward into successful, contented lives.

## PRAYER

*Father, it is so hard to remember that this is the work you have prepared for my hands. There are many days when I question this calling and shudder in frustration.*

*These precious ones that you have put in my care were chosen specifically for me. Help me to know their needs. Guide me as I make choices on their behalf. Grant me peace as I struggle through the obstacle course of school life. Soften the hearts of those who might hinder my work. Reveal to me those to whom I may also offer support. I am here because you put me here. Help me never to forget your Son's legacy as I leave my own.*

# 4
# *F*IRST TIMERS

## THE RIGHT WORDS

*Rejoice with those who rejoice; mourn with those who mourn.*
*Live in harmony with one another.*

ROMANS 12:15–16

## SPOKEN AT THE RIGHT TIME

True Christian love will enable us to take part in one another's sorrows and joys. It is not for us to say what should be rejoiced over and what should be grieved over. If we are to love as Christ loves us, we will not question whether or not something is important, but rather empathize fully with our brothers and sisters. We must work hard as much as it depends on us to be in unity with regard to spiritual truths, and when we have trouble doing that, to agree to disagree in love.

## BRING UNDERSTANDING AND PEACE

T eaching can quickly become mundane. Even beginning-of-the-school-year excitement can be lost on some of us. After all, we know what we're doing, we know what to expect, and we know the routine. But students and their parents new to our classes know none of these things.

Our younger son started middle school with trepidation, as do many new sixth graders. Having taught middle school myself, I recognized his deer-caught-in-the-headlights look as we entered the school. We arrived for our informal orientation on time and didn't see the teacher who would guide us through this foreign land. Finally she arrived, out of breath, talking at the speed of light, and not looking at us. We followed her hurried pace and barely heard her explanations on this so-called guided tour. Within minutes we were back at the front entrance and she absent-mindedly shook our hands, called my son by someone else's name, and disappeared down the hall. Whew!

Our son's mouth hung like an open mailbox, and his eyes stared in shock after the blur of a teacher. I know she didn't mean to be so impersonal. I know it was never her intention to treat us like the least important people on the planet. Nevertheless, this was our introduction to middle school.

We stayed awhile longer and matched his schedule to a map of the school I got from the office. We wandered the labyrinth of hallways and found each and every class. By the time we left, we were both more at ease about the first day of school. I couldn't vouch for the rest of the year, though!

## ONE HEART AT A TIME

Remember that the first day of school is just that—the first day for those in your care. They don't know you. They don't know what to expect. And most have some anxiety about it all. Be mindful of their needs and meet them when you can.

## PRAYER

*Lord, it is so easy for me to get caught up in the "every day" of teaching and forget the excitement, the anxiety, and the fear students and parents alike sometimes feel when they walk into a school. Make me sensitive to their feelings and meet them right where they are.*

# 5
# *E*XPECTATIONS

## THE RIGHT WORDS

*For everyone to whom much is given, from him much will be
required; and to whom much has been committed,
of him they will ask the more.*

LUKE 12:48 NKJV

## SPOKEN AT THE RIGHT TIME

We are not left ignorant about what Christ requires of us.
We should not only thirst after His Word so that we
might come to know more, but we are to take what He has
required and run with it.

Those around us who know that we are Christians will
have certain expectations. If their expectations are grounded
in God's truth, we would do well to go above and beyond
what is expected so that they can see that truth lived out in
our lives.

## BRING UNDERSTANDING AND PEACE

I couldn't believe I was finally here! One of my heart's desires has always been to teach teachers. Teaching the education program at a Christian college made my heart leap. This was where I belonged. This was a place that had high standards and a rigorous program. We would graduate teachers of excellence. Our children deserve the best.

One of my dearest friends had a similar dream. In fact, she started teaching at a Christian college in the education program as well. I couldn't wait to share our experiences, even though it was only through e-mail. We lived two thousand miles apart.

Joni became unusually quiet. My enthusiasm was one-sided. Finally she called and confessed her frustration.

"It's just not what I expected," she said almost in a whisper.

"What do you mean?" I asked.

"I know we're in a teacher shortage, but to pass people who barely complete the minimum requirements irks me!" her volume increased.

"And another thing," she said, gaining momentum. "What they require is less than I did during my first year in high school!"

"Have you—?" I began, but Joni was on a roll.

"It's a Christian school. Our standards should be some of the highest, not the lowest!" Joni took a breath and gave me just enough time to break in.

"Can you change it from where you sit?" I asked.

"No. I'm the low man on the totem pole," she said.

"If you can't maintain high standards where you are, then maybe it's time to leave," I said, knowing the magnitude of my advice.

"That's why I called. I gave my resignation this morning." Joni's voice trembled to the point of breaking.

## ONE HEART AT A TIME

We serve a God of excellence! Nothing He does is substandard. We have the Holy Spirit within us. There is no reason that what we do with the gifts He has given us should be anything short of excellent!

## PRAYER

*Lord Jesus, you were on earth, and through your Word continue to be my only reliable role model. Your lesson plans, now complete, enable me to follow them with a strong desire and due diligence to learn what I'm here to learn so that I might be able to better teach others.*

G iven the choice, you might be tempted to put aside the cares of the week in a box labeled "To Do Monday." Maybe instead you could take the contents of the box and one by one lay your cares at the foot of the cross. Give the name of each child in your care to our heavenly Father. Ask Him to care for them. Ask Him to protect them in and out of their homes. Ask Him to give you a sense of renewal so that you can again give your students what they need.

## INTO YOUR HANDS, LORD . . .

*Pray for*

_____

_____

_____

_____

_____

*Humble yourselves, therefore, under God's mighty hand, that he may lift you up in due time. Cast all your anxiety on him because he cares for you.*
1 PETER 5:6–7

# 6

# YOU ARE WHERE YOU BELONG

## THE RIGHT WORDS

*Nevertheless, each one should retain the place in life that the Lord assigned to him and to which God has called him. This is the rule I lay down in all the churches. Was a man already circumcised when he was called? He should not become uncircumcised. Was a man uncircumcised when he was called? He should not be circumcised. Circumcision is nothing and uncircumcision is nothing. Keeping God's commands is what counts. Each one should remain in the situation which he was in when God called him. Were you a slave when you were called? Don't let it trouble you—although if you can gain your freedom, do so. For he who was a slave when he was called by the Lord is the Lord's freedman; similarly, he who was a free man when he was called is Christ's slave. You were bought with a price; do not become slaves of men. Brothers, each man, as responsible to God, should remain in the situation God called him to.*

1 CORINTHIANS 7: 17–24

## SPOKEN AT THE RIGHT TIME

So often when we come to a saving belief in Jesus Christ and engage in a personal relationship with Him, life, which always seemed to be in varying shades of gray, becomes starkly black and white. We feel compelled to draw away from the world and to be separate. Yet what if you are exactly where you belong? What if God wants you right where you are so you can be His hands and feet to the people you work with?

This doesn't mean that we should never consider transferring to another school or leaving teaching altogether. It just means that we should bloom where we're planted!

## BRING UNDERSTANDING AND PEACE

My Christian walk started to gain speed about the time I graduated from college. Even though I attended public schools and all of my teacher preparation happened in public schools, I felt that I needed to leave them to teach in a Christian school. I believed it was the right thing to do. I wanted to teach with like-minded teachers and students who believed what I believed. So I requested that my final internship be conducted at a Christian school.

The beauty of this school surpassed my imagination. The classes were small. The facilities were spotless. The food was great! Each morning we met as a faculty and opened with prayer. It was so nice to be able to live what I believe in freedom. It seemed perfect—heavenly.

But we're not in heaven yet, are we? We're still here on earth where things are not perfect and people sin. By the end of the first week problems that I couldn't ignore surfaced from this seemingly perfect place. Many of the teachers were not certified. Students with special needs were ignored or encouraged to go elsewhere for an education. And since my degree was in special education, I couldn't pretend this didn't bother me. As my second week came to a close, I discovered that I had no decision-making power when it came to how to teach or discipline my students. I felt enslaved.

I went to my supervising professor at the university and asked to be transferred to a public school for the remaining fourteen weeks of my internship. She didn't say, "I told you so." She didn't even snicker. However, she did assign me to what was left—one of the most difficult high schools in the district. I humbly accepted the offer.

God had perfectly equipped me to teach in a public school. It was where He had "assigned" me all along. I just thought I knew better! As a Christian I was a good teacher in a public school. I believe now that's where I'm called to be. And I only want to be where God wants me to be.

## ONE HEART AT A TIME

Do you feel that you are all alone as the only Christian in your school? First, remember that God is in control. And second, it may not be that you're the *only* Christian—just the *first* Christian! A light is only as noticeable as the darkness it illuminates.

## PRAYER

*Lord, I want to be where you want me to be, doing what you want me to do. Please reveal to me whether I am where I belong. I can't trust my own motives, so let me know that I can go about your work right where I am.*

# 7
# COVER YOUR BASES

## THE RIGHT WORDS

*Finally, be strong in the Lord and in his mighty power. Put on the
full armor of God so that you can take your stand against the
devil's schemes. For our struggle is not against flesh and blood, but
against the rulers, against the authorities, against the powers of this
dark world and against the spiritual forces of evil in the heavenly
realms. Therefore put on the full armor of God, so that when the
day of evil comes, you may be able to stand your ground,
and after you have done everything, to stand.*

EPHESIANS 6:10–13

## SPOKEN AT THE RIGHT TIME

Putting on the whole armor of God is not a suggestion—
it is a command. We are in battle. We are soldiers. Soldiers prepare themselves for battle. School authorities tell us
that we should be prepared for the onslaught of criticism by

filling out forms in triplicate, having a witness attend any teacher/parent meeting, and never finding ourselves alone with a child. These are good suggestions, but they won't stop the Enemy.

We can, in full confidence, utilize the offensive weapon of prayer, claim the protection of the Word of God, and carry the sword of truth. It won't stop the arrows from flying at us, but they will not pierce us!

## BRING UNDERSTANDING AND PEACE

There are days when I don't want to admit to strangers that I am a teacher. Once people learn our profession they freely offer their opinion on the state of public education, the lousy teacher their daughter had in fourth grade, or how a principal didn't see that their darling son could never have hit the new kid on the playground. That's outside of school.

Inside of school there are just as many challenges, if not more. Students refuse to work, colleagues step on you to make themselves look better, and administrators force you to do things to make the school look good regardless of the cost to students. I know there are many good days in education, but the rest might feel like a losing battle. You feel like everyone is out to get you, and often you're right!

These are the moments when I struggle the most. For

some reason these are the times I forget the God I serve and look for ways to defend myself. But it isn't a defensive posture I need. It's an offensive one.

Teachers influence the minds of students. And Christian teachers have the added benefit of the power of the Holy Spirit. That is not lost on the Enemy. He will do whatever it takes to discourage and discredit us. We shouldn't be surprised, but we should be prepared.

## ONE HEART AT A TIME

When it seems as though you're surrounded by enemies, remember that your God has already won this fight. You can rest in the assurance that if you need defending, He will defend you. If you need protection, He will protect you. If you need courage, He will encourage you!

## PRAYER

*Almighty God and Father, I pray today for the confidence your Word provides. I pray that I will trust in the unfailing strength of the armor you've prepared for my use. It fits me perfectly and cannot be penetrated. Thank you for giving me all I need to fight the battle for the minds and souls of your children.*

# 8

# ROLL CALL PRAYER

## THE RIGHT WORDS

*I urge, then, first of all, that requests, prayers, intercession and thanksgiving be made for everyone—for kings and all those in authority, that we may live peaceful and quiet lives in all godliness and holiness. This is good, and pleases God our Savior, who wants all men to be saved and to come to a knowledge of the truth.*

1 TIMOTHY 2:1–4

## SPOKEN AT THE RIGHT TIME

How often do we pray for our principals, the school board, the superintendent, the state and federal legislators, and the taxpayers who can make or break our school budgets? Probably not often enough. We find ourselves at odds with many of these authorities when we are called to live "peaceful and quiet lives in all godliness and holiness."

We are called to make requests, prayers, intercession, and thanksgiving for those in authority over us. This is a practical way to take the focus off our own requests, trusting God with them, so that we can turn our attention to those who may not know Him personally.

The goal isn't to get what we want, but for God to get what He wants—all people to be saved and to come to the knowledge of the truth!

## BRING UNDERSTANDING AND PEACE

In disgust I threw the newspaper into the recycling bin. My husband is so good at leaving articles for me to read that have to do with teachers or education. However, it is rare if these articles tout good news. This day I read about new legislation concerning schools in our state. I shook my head in disbelief, wanting to scream! Everyone quoted in this article was a government official. Not one educator's opinion was sought.

I realized a long time ago that no one was going to ask my opinion about pending decisions regarding education. Somehow educators aren't consulted about the business of educating. It usually throws me into fits of frustration, and the only one who gets to hear my opinion is my always patient husband. For that I am quite grateful, but I keep waiting to be asked to testify before Congress about the state of American education!

Waiting is one thing, but it's not productive. The advocate in me wants to do something—something that will make a difference. And yet I feel helpless and ill-equipped to make any real difference. I ask God what we can do about those in authority who don't know what they're doing. "Remove them!" I plead. And in that moment I realize the truth. God is the one who appointed them in the first place.

Until the day when I am asked to testify, I will do what my God has called me to do. Make requests, pray specifically, and give thanks for those authorities He has placed in my life and the lives of all educators. I may not understand how it all works together. I may not grasp the vastness of His plan. But I am not helpless. I do have a voice that counts. I can lift that voice up to the ears that will hear—they're the only ears that matter anyway.

## ONE HEART AT A TIME

Every time you hear or read something that makes your skin crawl about what those in charge are going to do to change education—*pray!* If you heed that call, you'll be praying every day!

## PRAYER

*Lord, my habit has been to try to argue, manipulate, or depend upon my professionalism to change the hearts and minds of those in authority over me. Help me to break this habit and to learn yours instead. Let my mouth be full of prayers, praises, and thanksgiving for my principal, superintendent, and other leaders. Let them come to know you by first knowing me.*

# 9
# CHOOSE MERCY

## THE RIGHT WORDS

*But I tell you who hear me: Love your enemies, do good to those
who hate you, bless those who curse you, pray for those who
mistreat you. If someone strikes you on one cheek, turn to him the
other also. If someone takes your cloak, do not stop him from
taking your tunic. Give to everyone who asks you, and if anyone
takes what belongs to you, do not demand it back. Do to
others as you would have them do to you.*

*If you love those who love you, what credit is that to you? Even
"sinners" love those who love them. And if you do good to those
who are good to you, what credit is that to you? Even "sinners" do
that. And if you lend to those from whom you expect repayment,
what credit is that to you? Even "sinners" lend to "sinners,"
expecting to be repaid in full. But love your enemies, do good to
them, and lend to them without expecting to get anything back.
Then your reward will be great, and you
will be sons of the Most High, because he is kind
to the ungrateful and wicked.
Be merciful, just as your Father is merciful.*

LUKE 6: 27–36

## SPOKEN AT THE RIGHT TIME

Dealing with difficult people is part of the job of a teacher. The temptation is to take everything personally and then hold it against the parent or child in question (whether we're aware of it or not). There's also a tendency to extend kindness and mercy to those who can repay us with the same. What credit is that to us?

Could it be that we were placed intentionally by the Sovereign Lord in the lives of these children and their parents? The assignment, if we choose to accept it, is to love the unlovable and extend mercy to those least deserving of it. After all, isn't that what Jesus Christ has done for us?

## BRING UNDERSTANDING AND PEACE

David was difficult to deal with from day one. I called the first parent/teacher conference by the end of the third week of school. Nip it in the bud, I always say. I knew David was capable, and he was obviously talented, but he had a hard time following rules and it disrupted our class day after day. I knew if I could just get his parents to partner with me on this, we could draw out the talented David and slowly but surely calm the rebellious David.

During that conference I discovered where David's rebellion came from. His mother. She didn't even wait to hear the wonderful things I had to tell her about David's talents (what

I usually do before ever giving bad news). She jumped down my throat quicker than a bug during a bike ride!

"He's never had trouble before!" she said, raising her voice and herself out of the chair.

"You're the only one who's ever complained," she continued.

The conference lasted a total of four minutes. The only thing I said was, "David is quite bright."

"Then why did you call me down here?" she said, before slamming the door as she left.

Okay. Deep breaths. Think happy thoughts. And then I cried. I don't handle confrontation well.

The next day when I looked at David, all I could see and hear was his mother. I couldn't erase her words from my mind. The moment David started to wriggle in his seat I jumped on him to stay still. All day I was on the hunt for any and everything he might do wrong. He was quieter that day, but he did very little work. He turned to me as he left with a look of confused betrayal. What had I done?

It was easier for me to take out my frustration on this nine-year-old instead of on his mother. But it was wrong. His mother wasn't in my care day after day. David was. He didn't deserve my ill treatment of him, just as I didn't deserve his mother's ill treatment of me. I couldn't control his mom, but I knew I had to control myself.

*Forgive her,* the Spirit whispered.

The next day I asked David to forgive me. He did so gleefully. He had mercy that only humbled me. How could I hold a grudge against a child for his parent's actions?

## ONE HEART AT A TIME

You can't control what others do, but you can and must control your own actions. Holding grudges against students either because of their actions or those of their parents will change how you treat them, teach them, and lead them. Choose to lead through mercy. After all, we can forgive much because we have been forgiven much more!

## PRAYER

*Lord, I know you have forgiven me much. I know that I do not deserve your mercy and can never repay your kindness. Help me to give of myself without expecting repayment. Help me to love those who hate me, so that through me they might see you!*

# 10

# EXCESS BAGGAGE

## THE RIGHT WORDS

*Come to me, all you who are weary and burdened, and I will give
you rest. Take my yoke upon you and learn from me, for I am
gentle and humble in heart, and you will find rest for your souls.
For my yoke is easy and my burden is light.*

MATTHEW 11:28–30

## SPOKEN AT THE RIGHT TIME

Coming to Christ when in need is a choice, not forced
obedience. It is the only place we can truly find rest.
Christ *promises* rest! His commandments are holy, just, and
good. They may require that we deny ourselves in order to
follow them, but the reward is that of unconditional love.

Teachers are weary and brokenhearted people at times.
We need rest and renewal. But where we turn for the source
of our rest will determine whether or not we really find it.

Come to Him daily for relief from all your cares, fears, frustrations, and sorrows.

## BRING UNDERSTANDING AND PEACE

At times the burdens we feel as teachers equal the piles on our desks. They become heavy and unwieldy and sometimes too much to bear. I admit that many are simply a part of the job description and we must carry them. But there are so many others that we choose to pick up and add to our already heavy load; we need to learn to let go of those. Jesus said we should take His yoke upon us and His burden—for it is light. How can we take His burden if our hands are already full?

What do our own burdens look like? *Anger* as a result of getting our pride hurt. *An unforgiving spirit* toward a parent or colleague. *The desire to please others* to our own detriment. How many things do we say yes to just to please others? What about busyness with the motive to please others, or which merely reflects our personality? It could also be our past that gets in the way. What kinds of teachers did we have? Do we yell because our teachers yelled? All these things are excess baggage.

I know that I desperately want rest—I need rest! Yet I cannot find it. I want to believe Christ when He says His yoke is easy and His burden is light. I don't want to be a teacher people have to walk around as if on egg shells. I don't want my students to be afraid I will explode at any minute. I want joy. I want freedom from these unnecessary burdens. And I want everyone who knows me to see a happy, contented teacher.

We accumulate baggage along our journey toward becoming more and more like Christ. It gets in our way when we continually carry it with us. It takes time to unpack each burden and put things away. Only then can we carry Christ's burden. He died so that we wouldn't have to carry those extra bags anymore. Why do we choose to pick them up and take them with us anyway?

## ONE HEART AT A TIME

You can live an abundant life as a teacher today. It is a process that takes time, but it is worth every minute. Christ said we must learn from Him by taking His yoke upon ourselves. How did He do it when He was here on earth? Become His student and learn from the Master Teacher.

## PRAYER

*Heavenly Father, I am so tired. I cannot seem to find rest for my soul or my body. I must be looking in all the wrong places. I forget that you are the only true lasting source of rest. Welcome me under the shelter of your wings. Send your Comforter and give me peace.*

Are you weary and brokenhearted? Do you sense within yourself a desperate longing for rest? You can have it, dear one. You can find it. God created rest just for you and me! Spend more time getting to know your heavenly Father and you will feel your anxious heart become calm. Take each burden that is too heavy for you and let it fall by the wayside as you walk this journey of faith. Consider now what occupies more time and more energy than your relationship with God and pray that He will help you to release it from your tight grasp.

### INTO YOUR HANDS, LORD . . .

*Pray for*

_____

_____

_____

_____

_____

*Do not conform any longer to the pattern of this world, but be transformed by the renewing of your mind. Then you will be able to test and approve what God's will is—his good, pleasing and perfect will.*

ROMANS 12:2

# II

# $\mathscr{T}$HE TEACHABLE TEACHER

## THE RIGHT WORDS

*Who is wise? He will realize these things. Who is discerning? He will understand them. The ways of the Lord are right; the righteous walk in them, but the rebellious stumble in them.*

HOSEA 14:9

## SPOKEN AT THE RIGHT TIME

God is looking for teachable spirits. Those who want to learn His ways will learn. So often we look for ways to solve our problems outside of God's teaching. Instead, we rely on our own knowledge to find the answers.

But our ways are not reliable, and the information may be faulty. God's ways are right! We can trust where they will lead us. We must first acknowledge our depravity and then thirst after Wisdom. Only then will we find it.

## BRING UNDERSTANDING AND PEACE

When I first taught gifted middle school students, I was thrust into the assignment with only a few days' notice. Although I felt prepared having just finished my master's program in gifted education, I knew that in order for my students to learn, I had to stay one step ahead of them. Instead, I played catch-up for most of that first year.

Most of these kids were much smarter than I am. They came to class with questions for which I didn't have answers. That is a very humbling place to be as a teacher. And then when their parents questioned my credentials, I knew I had to do something in order to win their confidence.

Step one—put my pride aside and be willing to learn. It's hard to accept that as the grown-up I don't have all the answers. But my desire to be the best teacher I could be to these students motivated me to become a better learner.

Step two—admit when I don't know an answer and strive to find it.

"Why didn't NASA continue its manned space program to the moon?" one especially precocious sixth-grader asked me.

"I honestly don't know," I said. "But we can e-mail them and ask."

Children need to learn to think for themselves. But so do adults. I didn't have a teacher's manual for these classes. It was a matter of determining what I knew, what I needed to know, and how to find out what I needed to know. That made it safe for my students to admit to what they didn't know (not easy for a gifted youngster) and be willing to look for the answers themselves.

## ONE HEART AT A TIME

You don't have to be the perfect teacher with all the answers to win the hearts and minds of your students. You just have to be teachable yourself.

## PRAYER

*Lord God, your Spirit lives within me and it thirsts after you! I pant after you and long to drink at the well of Living Water. Your water is free from impurities and quenches my thirst like nothing else!*

# 12
# ꟿoy Stealers

## THE RIGHT WORDS

*Unless the Lord had given me help, I would soon have dwelt in the silence of death. When I said, "My foot is slipping," your love, O Lord, supported me. When anxiety was great within me, your consolation brought joy to my soul.*

PSALM 94:17–19

## SPOKEN AT THE RIGHT TIME

The psalmist reveals his inability to save himself. He admits to feeling great anxiety and even fear at the task ahead. Not knowing where or how his call would end, he struggled to find relief or rest with those around him. Left to his own devices, he would surely fall.

God knows that we will experience trial and trouble. He knows we will walk around with anxious thoughts and troubled hearts. But do we know that He is the only one who can steady a stumbling foot or calm a concerned mind? We can still experience the joy of our calling if we allow God to carry the burdens that calling presents.

## BRING UNDERSTANDING AND PEACE

I know I was called to teach. It was obvious from my earliest memories of sitting my four siblings down with paper and pencil and teaching them something. I was made for this! It is a joyful thing to know that you are doing what you were made to do. But there are a litany of things that occupy my mind and even my prayers that squeeze the joy out of my calling.

Where am I going to find the time to go through every student's cumulative file and check that all the testing results are there? This is the second time this month we've had to check for head lice—will we ever get past this problem? The new language arts textbook may be pretty, but there aren't enough of them for each child to have his own. Danny still doesn't know his addition facts. He's the only one who is still working on this. Is that bruise on Sandy's cheek really from falling off her bike? How am I going to finish this paper work and get home in time to make dinner for my family? On and on it goes . . . where it stops, nobody knows.

Not only do I feel my foot slipping, it feels as if I'm slipping off the edge of a cliff and into an abyss.

It is a daily choice to lift my hands up to the only One who can steady my footing and carry me over the abyss that seems to always wait for me. It doesn't mean that I won't have to check heads for lice or deal with the mountain of paper work in a limited time. It means that I can choose to let God carry those burdens for me in my thoughts and prayers so that there's room for the joy promised with this calling.

## ONE HEART AT A TIME

Is your foot hovering over the edge of worry and anxiety that do nothing but steal your joy? Stop trying to handle it all yourself, and cry out to your heavenly Father. He is waiting to be your knight in shining armor!

## PRAYER

*Loving Father, the burden of my calling to teach is about to crush me like a steamroller. I can't find the joy I once had. I can't see where this will end. I look into a great abyss and fear for my future. Save me, O Lord. Grant me what I need to faithfully continue in this calling to teach your children.*

# 13
# $V$ETERANS

## THE RIGHT WORDS

*The righteous shall flourish like a palm tree,*
*He shall grow like a cedar in Lebanon.*
*Those who are planted in the house of the Lord*
*Shall flourish in the courts of our God.*
*They shall still bear fruit in old age;*
*They shall be fresh and flourishing,*
*To declare that the Lord is upright;*
*He is my rock, and there is no unrighteousness in Him.*

PSALM 92:12–15 NKJV

## SPOKEN AT THE RIGHT TIME

A life lived faithfully following God is a life that bears fruit, even in our last years, months, moments. Perseverance is the mark of a sincere believer. It is so easy to be on fire and go about God's work in the beginning of our walk. But as time goes on, the obstacles are many and the rewards few.

It isn't a matter of how much money we earn or if we are praised with ceremonial honors or awards. Rather, it is a matter of whether we can continue to praise the name of the Lord and say "He is good!" no matter what our circumstances. We are carefully watched by both the faithful and the unfaithful. They will know about God's faithfulness by witnessing our own, even until our retirement day and beyond.

## BRING UNDERSTANDING AND PEACE

He's been teaching for forty-two years!" my friend exclaimed. "He says he's retiring this year, but I'm so grateful he's here now."

"I hope Griffon gets what he needs out of that math class, though," I worried. "Some teachers should have left the classroom a long time ago."

"Not this one," she said. "He works these kids hard and says they won't leave his classroom until they know all fourteen operations. That's what Griffon needs."

Mr. Murphy wasn't concerned about the new state standards or the newly adopted math curriculum. He knew how to teach and to ensure his students got what they needed. It's a magical sort of mystery how some teachers always know just what to do to get kids to learn. *He must be tired*, I thought. *He must be less on his game than when he first started*. But the fire in his belly to make a difference in the lives of children still burned as hot as ever.

The call to teach supercedes all boundaries, walls, and ill-defined pathways. We can cross those borders, climb the walls, and mark out our own paths, if that's what it takes to do what we've been called to do. And it doesn't stop being a calling when we've taught for thirty or more years. A teacher teaches—always.

## ONE HEART AT A TIME

The veteran has much to offer the novice. As the novice, seek the knowledge and expertise of the veteran. As the veteran, continue to bear fruit no matter how long you've taught or how many years, months, or days you have until retirement. Sometimes the best work we do is in our last year in the classroom.

## PRAYER

*Lord, hold me up with your right hand. Equip me to do your work to the end of my days. Grant me the strength and desire to follow you until my last breath. Let my mouth praise your name forever to all those around me. Help me to persevere even when I am old and weary of body.*

# 14

# HOPELESSLY DEVOTED

## THE RIGHT WORDS

*Later, knowing that all was now completed, and so that the
Scripture would be fulfilled, Jesus said, "I am thirsty." A jar of
wine vinegar was there, so they soaked a sponge in it, put the
sponge on a stalk of the hyssop plant, and lifted it to Jesus' lips.
When he had received the drink, Jesus said, "It is finished."
With that, he bowed his head and gave up his spirit.*

JOHN 19:28–30

## SPOKEN AT THE RIGHT TIME

When Jesus uttered his last words, "It is finished," he
meant it. He had done all that was expected of him. All
prophesies were fulfilled. The law was fulfilled. The work of
the Father was completed. Jesus had an incredible "to do" list
and He was able to check off each and every task.

Christ is the creator and finisher of our faith. He has

already overcome the world. He is the beginning and the end. Our hope lies in Him alone and not in our own ability to get the job done. We may never feel as if we have finished everything on our "to do" list, even at the end of our life, but in God's eyes it will be finished nevertheless.

## BRING UNDERSTANDING AND PEACE

I hope I don't have any major behavior problems this year." "I hope our new principal realizes the talented staff he has."

"I hope we get a cost of living increase this year."

"I hope I don't run out of copy paper before the end of the year again."

"I hope my students do well on the state test."

I hope, I hope, I hope. We define a successful school year by these hopes and more. And we are often disappointed and discouraged. There's nothing wrong with these hopes in and of themselves. But they are bound to let us down. We don't have control over any of them.

As Christian teachers we can't depend upon these hopes. They may or may not come to pass. If they don't, we can still have hope. And others around us will want to know why.

So if we run out of supplies, have more than our share of discipline problems, and are blamed for everything wrong in education, we can still have hope because we know that our

real hope is not in the things of this world, but in the world
to come.

## ONE HEART AT A TIME

Our real hope is that Christ lives within us, so that we are
now able to be His hands and feet to the families in our
care. How we teach can bring the hope of Christ to others.
Isn't that what it's all about?

## PRAYER

*Lord God, Heavenly King, Almighty God and Father,
you are the beginner and finisher of my faith! Let me
walk daily in the assurance of the hope of your Son. When
I am overwhelmed, help me not to be overcome by the tasks
of this job. Let your hope shine from within me to all those
around me and let them be drawn to you by the sheer
beauty of your Word.*

# 15
# An Act to Follow

## THE RIGHT WORDS

*That the generation to come might know them, even the children*
*which should be born; who should arise and declare them to their*
*children: that they might set their hope in God, and not forget the*
*works of God, but keep his commandments: and might not be as*
*their fathers, a stubborn and rebellious generation; a generation*
*that set not their heart aright, and whose spirit*
*was not steadfast with God.*

PSALM 78:6–8 KJV

## SPOKEN AT THE RIGHT TIME

Our goal should be to set godly examples for our students. They will learn about God's goodness, His wondrous works, and His unending grace through those who teach them, whether we are their parents or their schoolteachers. Let us not copy the sinful or rebellious actions of those who do not follow God, even if that was the only example set for us. We can choose instead to follow God, for His example was set through his Son.

## BRING UNDERSTANDING AND PEACE

When Sally Barker became our middle school's new principal, her reputation preceded her. She was known throughout our county as an excellent administrator—a real professional, but who still remembered what it meant to be in the classroom. I was excited! I saw this as a chance for me to grow as a teacher. To be under her wings was an honor.

Sally had a tough job ahead of her. She had a disinterested and disenfranchised faculty to mold into a topnotch, professional teaching machine. If you didn't want to come on board, you'd be left behind. I was proud that she was our principal. At area meetings, people would say upon hearing where I taught, "Oh, you're one of Sally's teachers. It's very nice to meet you!"

We like to hang around those with the best reputations. And if someone is of ill repute, we should stay far away from her. Our own reputations are elevated or tainted by those of the leaders we follow.

I'm so glad that God doesn't operate this way. Actually, we don't have a human relationship to remind us of what our heavenly Father thinks of us. We want to be a part of Him because of His perfect reputation. But when we look at our own deeds, we're ashamed and wonder how He could possibly be proud to be called our God! It's pretty humbling.

## ONE HEART AT A TIME

No matter the reputation of those you associate with, choose to follow the one true God, whose ways are always worthy of praise and whose reputation is above reproach.

## PRAYER

*Lord, God, walking in this world requires an incredible amount of discernment. There are those who desire to catch me in a snare, and there are those who boldly seek to destroy my reputation. Give me discernment to recognize your good deeds in those around me and to make the right choices of action by which to pattern my life. That way the children in my charge can trust what they see in me.*

Teachers are in the people-pleasing business. Unfortunately, when people aren't as pleased with us as we think they ought to be, we become painfully aware of the fact that we are not in control. Our desire to please our administrators, colleagues, parents, and even students can end up debilitating us instead. May we desire to please the one who truly is in control of it all—our heavenly Father. Consider those whom you've strived to please. Commit them and their needs to God.

### INTO YOUR HANDS, LORD . . .

*Pray for*

_____

_____

_____

_____

_____

*You therefore, my son, be strong in the grace that is in Christ Jesus. And the things that you have heard from me among many witnesses, commit these to faithful men who will be able to teach others also. You therefore must endure hardship as a good soldier of Jesus Christ.*

2 TIMOTHY 2:1–3 NKJV

# 16

# CHEERLEADER BARNABAS

## THE RIGHT WORDS

*News of this reached the ears of the church at Jerusalem, and they sent Barnabas to Antioch. When he arrived and saw the evidence of the grace of God, he was glad and encouraged them all to remain true to the Lord with all their hearts. He was a good man, full of the Holy Spirit and faith, and a great number of people were brought to the Lord.*

ACTS 11:22–24

## SPOKEN AT THE RIGHT TIME

B arnabas was a man of faith and his encouragement to those who preached the gospel was the fruit of his faith. He was excited at the Lord's success through the apostles who went to Antioch. He rejoiced with those who rejoice.

Some teachers have more success with their students than others. Sometimes a child you worked tirelessly with doesn't show improvement until after he leaves you and works with another teacher. How does that make you feel? We can be happy for the Lord's success through another teacher. We can encourage others in their quest to educate and inspire even when we are on sabbatical. Look for ways to be a Barnabas in the lives of others.

## BRING UNDERSTANDING AND PEACE

I always wanted to be a cheerleader. Yet in my heart I knew that I wanted it for all the wrong reasons. I wanted their perfect, perky bodies and their clear skin and smiles. I wanted to be like them because everyone wanted to be like them. If you were a cheerleader, take no offense. I'm in awe of you to this day! A cheerleader's enthusiasm is contagious. That's her power; that's her role.

As a teacher I felt like a cheerleader at times. I tried desperately to cheer my students on to success—even when they were the underdogs and their success would be an upset. I never felt like I was sitting on the sidelines. I believed, and still do, that my role was important.

Now that I am no longer in the classroom, it's easy to think that I am sitting on the bench while the other teachers play the game and score the winning points. But that's a lie—

a lie that the Enemy would have me believe to make me ineffective for the kingdom. For a while I felt as I did in junior high when I would have traded my defiant red hair and freckles for the coveted cheerleader skirt and pompons.

The gift of encouragement doesn't end at the school doors. It is a part of God's design for many of us. When I hear of teachers who do good, I not only rejoice, but I tell them what a wonderful job they are doing. I want, more than anything, for others to catch my excitement and enthusiasm for the wonderful work of teachers, especially those who love the Lord. I am a cheerleader—a cheerleader of teachers. It's what I do. It makes me happy to do it. I think God might give me pompons when I get to heaven!

ONE HEART AT A TIME

Don't believe the adage *Those who can't, teach.* Believe instead, *Those who can't teach encourage those who do.*

## PRAYER

*Lord, give me a heart of encouragement. Let my faith be visible to all by the joy I experience on their behalf. Let no grain of jealousy exist in my being. Grant me the words to sustain the weary.*

# 17

# $\mathcal{A}$ WORKMAN APPROVED

## THE RIGHT WORDS

*Keep reminding them of these things. Warn them before God against quarreling about words; it is of no value, and only ruins those who listen. Do your best to present yourself to God as one approved, a workman who does not need to be ashamed and who correctly handles the word of truth. Avoid godless chatter, because those who indulge in it will become more and more ungodly. Their teaching will spread like gangrene.*

2 TIMOTHY 2:14–17

## SPOKEN AT THE RIGHT TIME

As we gather together (especially women) it is a temptation to gossip. A teacher's lounge is notorious for "godless chatter." God has carefully equipped us for the work He prepared for our hands. It is up to us to act in accordance with His equipping.

We must speak and act in a way that leaves us unashamed. If we habitually engage in godless chatter, we will become ungodly and our witness will suffer. Focus on the careful handling of God's truth, whether talking to students or fellow teachers.

## BRING UNDERSTANDING AND PEACE

I can't count the times I found myself engaged in gossip at school. My ears pricked up the moment I heard someone's name mentioned. But it made me wonder what was said when *I* wasn't there.

I don't handle confrontation well, so when I sat at lunch and heard my colleagues go on about how the new principal just wasn't their cup of tea, I sat silently eating my lunch. I was grateful no one asked my opinion. But inside I was anxious for the lunch hour to be over so I could return to the sanctuary of my classroom.

After a few more such sessions, I stopped eating lunch in the teachers' lounge and ate in my classroom instead. That way I wouldn't have to hear the gossip or feel compelled to dispel it. After all, I liked our new principal.

Escape was only temporary as I stumbled into a conversation bordering on the ones I had been avoiding in the teacher work room.

"She certainly thinks she's God's gift!" one said with venom.

"I've heard she left her last principalship because she was forced out," another said.

"Her husband's a principal too. I'm sure he's part of the reason she's at this school."

"Well, I'm not following the lead of someone who'll probably lead us off a cliff!" the first replied.

Something told me to stop.

"Do you know why she left her last school?"

The dreaded confrontation was upon me.

"No," I said. "And it doesn't matter. She's the one in charge. It's my job to follow her lead."

At that I returned to my classroom and slipped in the door just before the bell rang. Safe and sound in my sanctuary!

## ONE HEART AT A TIME

Some of us have been given the gift of teaching—not only to teach children, but to teach others God's Word. Even in the day-to-day world of a school, there will be opportunities to speak God's truth into the lives of others. Handle it carefully and prayerfully and do not be ashamed!

## PRAYER

*Lord, forgive me if my tongue has wandered away from your Word and praising your name. Help me to focus on the careful handling of your Word so that not only will I not be ashamed but your name will not be tarnished.*

# 18

# *H*OW DEEP IS HIS LOVE?

## THE RIGHT WORDS

*For this reason I kneel before the Father, from whom his whole family in heaven and on earth derives its name. I pray that out of his glorious riches he may strengthen you with power through his Spirit in your inner being, so that Christ may dwell in your hearts through faith. And I pray that you, being rooted and established in love, may have power, together with all the saints, to grasp how wide and long and high and deep is the love of Christ, and to know this love that surpasses knowledge—that you may be filled to the measure of all the fullness of God.*

EPHESIANS 3:14–19

## SPOKEN AT THE RIGHT TIME

Paul's passion about the love of Christ is hard to ignore in this passage. He knew how discouraged we become when faced with trials. The church at Ephesus became discouraged by Paul's trials and imprisonment. If they were to become so discouraged at his trials, how would they respond to their own, which were surely to come?

Paul used vivid language to describe the lengths and depths of Christ's love for us. He prayed that we would have this same understanding. God's love isn't given to us in part—we receive its fullness! In the midst of all that troubles us, can we know how deep and how wide God, the Creator of the universe, loves us? Yes, we can.

## BRING UNDERSTANDING AND PEACE

Sometimes it feels like I can't do anything right. I know I can't please everyone, but some days I feel like I can't please anyone! My four-year-old cried beyond consolation when I dropped him off at his preschool before going to work. He sat at the window with his little hands pressed against the glass, screaming silently at me as I pulled out of the driveway. I cried all the way to school.

At school my mailbox was full to bursting. I hadn't had time the day before to even make it up to the office to check it. Buried within the pile of papers like a needle in a haystack was a message from an irate parent, who by now would be even angrier because I hadn't responded to her message the day before. I sighed in defeat, and it was only 8:15 A.M.!

I walked into the faculty meeting late, distracted by all the messages I had to return, and met the cold stare of my principal as I sat down. With no rest for the weary, I then filed out of the auditorium with the rest of my colleagues and secluded myself in my classroom until my students showed up. Thank goodness, I had first period for planning.

I looked around the room and noticed small dots of white littering the gray carpet. What is that? Then it hit me. We had done an activity yesterday that required paper punches. Now my classroom was covered with white confetti. Why hadn't the custodian vacuumed? Just then Frank popped in and answered my unspoken question. "Next time stack the chairs, and then I'll vacuum."

By the time the day ended I had ten strikes against me. I left feeling discouraged, defeated, and desperate for acceptance. I couldn't wait to pick up my son. He would at least welcome me with open arms. But he didn't. He was cranky, and then I realized he had a fever. I'd have to take another sick day tomorrow. Great. Just what I needed—the secretary on my case for being out again.

Talk about running on empty! But I realized that this is exactly where God wanted me. Emptied of self-sufficiency, I could now go to the Living Water and be filled with the unsurpassed measure of God's love for me. It was unfathomable. I couldn't grasp the immensity of it. But I could choose to immerse myself in it and weep at the feet of the Father who loves me whether I stack the chairs or not.

## ONE HEART AT A TIME

How wide, how long, how high, and how deep is the love of God for His children? When your students don't listen and your principal disapproves of a choice you've made and parents protest your authority, know, without a doubt, that you are loved! Let a smile crease your face and wrap around the truth of the depths of His love for you!

## PRAYER

*Jesus Christ, lover of my soul, impress on me the depth of your love. I so easily forget how your love is unfailing and how it sustains me. Help me to focus instead on how you sacrificed yourself for my sake and how that greatest expression of love lives within me today. Let me be able to share that love with those who surround me and hold in my heart the deepest affection of your Spirit.*

# 19
# CALLED TO BE KIND

## THE RIGHT WORDS

*He who despises his neighbor sins, but blessed
is he who is kind to the needy.*

PROVERBS 14:21

## SPOKEN AT THE RIGHT TIME

The territorial nature of many teachers makes it hard for us to reach out to our teaching neighbors. We are all in need. We are all struggling. We are all alone. And yet we rarely reach out to one another. If we stay in our own little worlds, behind the closed doors of our classrooms, we will miss the blessing.

If we scorn or look down on the teacher next to us, for whatever reason, we sin. He or she may be the exact opposite in teaching style or temperament, but we are called to be kind and extend a hand of friendship.

## BRING UNDERSTANDING AND PEACE

The roar of the classroom next door reverberated through the sliding metal wall between us and interrupted my students who were working quietly. Some of the kids looked up at me for either an explanation or a solution—neither of which I could provide. Mr. Sanborn either was having way too much fun in his room or he didn't know how to control his students. Either way, they made it difficult once again for my students to work.

Mr. Sanborn was well loved by his students. He was the favorite teacher of many. But day by day I began to allow a root of bitterness to grow inside me. I was annoyed at his lack of classroom management, his disregard for the needs of surrounding classrooms, and his happy-go-lucky attitude that looked like he didn't care. I tried letting him know politely that his class was disruptive, but he just shrugged it off, believing he could win me over with his boyish charm.

I was tired of telling my students to simply ignore the racket next door. I was tired of being polite. Then suddenly the zoo-like sounds next door stopped. For three days it was quiet. Just in time too. I was about to go to the principal and formally complain. Then on day four the noise level escalated once again. I groaned and decided Mr. Sanborn was out of chances.

When I left the principal's office, I couldn't run out of the building fast enough. I needed to find a private place to fall apart. My principal gently answered my complaint about Mr. Sanborn with some startling news. The man was dying. An inoperable brain tumor was cutting short the career of a gifted teacher. Gifted teacher? I didn't understand. All I ever saw was a man who didn't have control over his classroom and didn't seem to understand how that affected the rest of us.

"He wanted as much time with his kids as possible," the principal explained. "I know he was struggling, but being with his students meant so much to him. I didn't want to cut that time short when the tumor was already cutting his life short."

Mr. Sanborn was in hospice now. The racket I heard that day was because the kids were testing the substitute. How could I have been so judgmental, so empty of grace, and so sure of myself? He was my teaching neighbor, after all!

The next day I went into his classroom for a few minutes to encourage his students in the loss of their beloved teacher. I opened myself up to their needs and invited them to visit next door whenever they wanted to. Only a couple of students took me up on that offer, but it was a kindness I extended. I prayed it wasn't too little too late.

## ONE HEART AT A TIME

Is there a teacher who is driving you crazy? I know your
first inclination is probably to distance yourself and shake
your head in disgust or disapproval. Yet we are called to
be kind. Look for real ways today to extend
kindness to your neighbor.

### PRAYER

*Lord, I struggle with feelings of bitterness toward
another teacher in our school. Right now I ask your
forgiveness, because I know that if I hate him, your Word
says I don't love you. I am miserable. Heal my spirit and
help me to extend a hand of kindness toward the most
unlovable.*

# 20
# *V*ICTORY!

## THE RIGHT WORDS

*I have brought you glory on earth by completing
the work you gave me to do.*

JOHN 17:4

## SPOKEN AT THE RIGHT TIME

Jesus said these words as He prayed to the Father before
He was arrested. He prayed first for himself, then for His
disciples, and finally for all believers. But these words are a
reminder to us that first, Jesus' focus was on glorifying His
Father in heaven and second, we should have the same focus.

We are all doing the work God gave us to do whether we
realize it or not. Our focus must be to bring God glory as we
complete that work. Our goals, our hopes, and all of our tasks
can be accomplished with this in mind: God's glory and not
our own.

## BRING UNDERSTANDING AND PEACE

A teacher's job is never done. The paper work waits for us each and every morning like a dog waiting to be walked. There is always one more thing on our "to do" list that never seems to get checked off. And children's needs are never completely met, no matter how hard we try.

I always took work home evenings and weekends. Homework to be graded, projects to go through, and upcoming lessons to plan all ate away at my free time. The needs and fears about my students even invaded my dreams. I've woken up crying on more than one occasion. Then suddenly the end of the school year looms and we run out of time—out of time to make a difference. If I focus too much on what still needs to be done, I'll sink into depression.

We have to be so careful that we don't look for our hope in what we may accomplish as an educator. We will never reach every child. We will never finish all that is required of us. We will never change the minds of our critics. Then where is the victory? Where is the hope?

On the cross Jesus said, "It is finished." He is the beginning and finisher of our faith. Even when we despair that our work will never be done in this world, we can have the hope that transcends the entire world's work. Instead of relying on our teaching expertise to change the lives of students, we can fix our hope on the unrivaled expertise of our Lord. Our real hope is that Christ lives within us, so that we can become the hands and feet of Christ daily to our students.

## ONE HEART AT A TIME

Glory be to the Father, and to the Son, and to the Holy Spirit.... The glory given to a job well done belongs to these three—the Trinity. If we are praised, the praise belongs to God. Even in the midst of a challenging school year, we can offer our work up to the glory of God.

### PRAYER

*Lord Jesus, even before you were given over to death, a death you freely accepted, you gave glory to God the Father. Help me in the midst of the good, the bad, and even the ugly to offer praise and thanksgiving. My good is God's glory!*

There are times when as a teacher we are on center stage. This is "my" classroom. These are "my" kids. We slowly, but surely, become very territorial. Once territory is established, we find ourselves protecting that territory in a variety of ways. We might close our door and put construction paper over the door's window (if we have one). We might eat lunch only with teachers who agree with our boundaries. We might look at an idea for "improvement" as an invasion of our privacy and put guards on our hearts—all under the guise of protecting our students, when in reality we are trying to protect ourselves.

Hold loosely those things that God has put in your charge. They are only on loan. We can protect them and set them apart, but only for God's glory, not our own. Consider those attitudes and actions that reveal your territorial nature and allow the Holy Spirit to work on behalf of "His" children.

## INTO YOUR HANDS, LORD . . .

*Pray for*

_____

_____

_____

*Trust in the Lord with all your heart,*
*And lean not on your own understanding;*
*In all your ways acknowledge Him,*
*And He shall direct your paths.*
PROVERBS 3:5–6 NKJV

# 21

# *T*HE LIBERTY OF GIVING!

## THE RIGHT WORDS

*This service that you perform is not only supplying the needs of
God's people but is also overflowing in many expressions of thanks
to God. Because of this service by which you have proved
yourselves, men will praise God for the obedience that accompanies
your confession of the gospel of Christ, and for your generosity
in sharing with them and with everyone else.*

2 CORINTHIANS 9:12–13

## SPOKEN AT THE RIGHT TIME

Charity is a form of love. In fact, the words are inter-
changeable in 2 Corinthians. We are called to share our
time, talents, and treasures with those in need. Some of those
in need are in our classrooms. Others are outside our direct

influence and so we offer our treasure to meet their needs.

"We must show the reality of our subjection to the gospel, by works of charity. This will be for the credit of our profession, and to the praise and glory of God. Let us endeavor to copy the example of Christ, being unwearied in doing good, and deeming it more blessed to give than to receive."[1]

## BRING UNDERSTANDING AND PEACE

I t was the very first day of school. I couldn't believe they wanted my money even before I received my first paycheck of the school year. I knew that the United Way did wonderful things for our communities, but I wasn't convinced that I should give to them. So many questions swirled through my mind. Would my money go to an organization that didn't match my beliefs or values? Would it go to administration costs instead of the hands of the needy? How much was the minimum gift? I couldn't really afford more than the minimum. We barely had enough to buy groceries. Charity begins at home, doesn't it?

I let a week go by without deciding. Then a banner appeared in the teacher work room. *100% Donation Incentives!* Following was a list of things ranging from early release on Fridays to gift certificates to a local restaurant. Were they bribing us to donate? I let another week go by.

Finally I was called into the principal's office on the last day of the campaign.

"Have you had a chance to turn in your donation envelope?" Mrs. Stable asked.

"No. I haven't decided what I'm going to do yet," I said.

"Today is the last day for 100 percent donation credit. Do you think you could turn your envelope in by the end of the day?" There was expectancy in her voice that made me uncomfortable.

By nature I am a compliant person. I follow the rules. I do what I am told. I am a giving person. I just don't like feeling coerced to give. How could I approach this God's way? It wasn't as if I were giving to a Christian ministry or mission. Was I really obligated to give? And if so, could I do it with a happy spirit?

"Each man should give what he has decided in his heart to give, not reluctantly or under compulsion, for God loves a cheerful giver" (2 Corinthians 9:7).

"I want to give to a specific organization under the United Way instead of to the United Way in general," I said to my principal with full confidence.

"No problem," she said. "It's an option on your donation form."

What a relief! Since I had avoided the whole issue for two weeks, I hadn't even looked at the donation form. God had already supplied a way for me to give in a way that I thought would please Him.

# ONE HEART AT A TIME

The call to give doesn't come only from our superiors. It comes directly from God. We should be known by our charity, for God is known through us.

### PRAYER

*My God, you take care of my needs—sometimes through the comfort of your Spirit within me, other times through the hands and feet of others. Your providence never falters. Help me to become your representative. Spur me on to do works of charity so that those whose needs I meet, meet you!*

# 22

# POWER STRUGGLE

## THE RIGHT WORDS

*Love is patient, love is kind. It does not envy, it does not boast, it is not proud. It is not rude, it is not self-seeking, it is not easily angered, it keeps no record of wrongs.*

1 CORINTHIANS 13:4–5

## SPOKEN AT THE RIGHT TIME

Giving the gift of love proves our faith. There's a song that says, "And they'll know we are Christians by our love." But what does love look like? How does it act?

Within our schools we can always find opportunities to show love. The list noted in 1 Corinthians 13:4–5 should be taken to heart. These character traits are part of the yardstick that measures whether or not we have the grace of love. If we don't, then we must strive to attain it.

## BRING UNDERSTANDING AND PEACE

How could someone less than four feet tall make me feel so small? Second-grader Tim Matthews and I went head to head every day beginning on the first day of school. There's always one who knows how to push all your buttons, and Tim certainly knew what to do to make me crazy.

In the beginning I was able to contain my discipline of him in a private manner—in the hall, at my desk, and so on. But his defiance bled out into the open and in plain view of the rest of the class. That was the moment the stakes were raised. I couldn't afford to look weak in front of twenty-eight other second-graders—not if I was to maintain control of my class.

I decided preventive measures were in order. They say the best defense is a good offense. I wanted to nip his defiant behavior in the bud. I wanted to get in the first punch. I was on the hunt for any sign of weakness like a lioness tracking a herd of gazelle. I wanted to win. After all, I'm the grown-up.

I felt secure in both my desire to regain control and my methods for doing so. I planned to watch him like a hawk and swoop down at the first sign of trouble. In my exuberance to take control of the situation I'd forgotten to commit my plans to the Lord. Then during my morning quiet time I prayed that today would be the day I'd have everything I needed to get control of this boy.

And God said . . . "You need to love him instead."

And I said, "How can I love him, Lord, when I don't even like him?"

"Practice, practice, practice," God's Word said to me in 1 Corinthians 13.

> *Vicki is patient. Vicki is kind. Vicki does not envy, she does not boast, she is not proud. Vicki is not rude, she is not self-seeking; she is not easily angered and keeps no account of wrongs. Vicki does not delight in evil but rejoices with the truth. She always protects, always hopes, always perseveres.*

In that moment my eyes were opened to the truth of my calling as a teacher. I wasn't called to prod children like cattle in the way I wanted them to go. I was called to love them first and teach them second. When Tim walked into my room the next morning I had a smile for him—the first one he'd seen all year. There's always one—one who will help you practice the gift of God's love.

ONE HEART AT A TIME

Is there a student who is a thorn in your side? He may be just the incentive you need to put your love for God and His love for this child into practice. Remember, practice makes perfect.

## PRAYER

*Lord, it is a daily challenge to love the unlovable. Help me to be a conduit of your love. Love them through me. Let my reputation always be one of charity and mercy!*

# 23
# *i* DON'T CARE SYNDROME

## THE RIGHT WORDS

*Never be lacking in zeal, but keep your spiritual fervor, serving the Lord. Be joyful in hope, patient in affliction, faithful in prayer.*

ROMANS 12:11–12

## SPOKEN AT THE RIGHT TIME

Zeal helps us to care when we don't feel like it, try when we don't really want to, and persevere when all we want to do is quit. But it's not a magical potion we can swallow—it is a work of the heart. Paul tells us in his letter to the Romans that we must be joyful in hope—the hope of God's kingdom to come; patient in affliction—wait patiently even when teaching is difficult at best and painful at most; and faithful in prayer—put everything of the school day at the foot of God's throne. Zeal is the result of these faithful works of the heart.

## BRING UNDERSTANDING AND PEACE

When I hear that someone has taught for thirty years I get nervous. I worry that she has overstayed her welcome and can't possibly still be enthusiastic about teaching. I equate youth with enthusiasm and excitement. I also tend to equate age with burnout and apathy.

I homeschooled our two boys for four years. When our younger son went back into public school there were a number of things that made me anxious. Discovering that his new fourth-grade teacher had taught in the system for thirty-one years didn't put my mind at ease. Charles himself hesitated the first day he met Mrs. Kammer. His first impression had him believing she was overly strict, mean, and most likely no fun at all. I was afraid she was too set in her ways to ever meet the unique needs of my son now entering public school for the first time since kindergarten.

By the end of the first week it was quite obvious that we were both wrong!

Joan Kammer is one of those incredible teachers who strives every day to be the best she can be for the sake of her students. She participated in school improvement, offered her expertise to state committees, and mentored younger, less experienced teachers. Her love for her students permeated how she planned her lessons, how she dealt with behavior, and how she rewarded every effort, no matter how small.

Admittedly, there are plenty of teachers out there who should have retired long ago and who are doing more harm than good. Their "I don't care anymore" attitude influences their planning, discipline, and incentives for their students. They have lost their zeal for teaching. Without zeal we can't give our best to our students.

Mrs. Kammer had zeal!

## ONE HEART AT A TIME

Zeal for serving the Lord is something we cultivate day by day, not something we wait for like lightning to strike.

## PRAYER

*Lord, I am so very tired. I know that you sustain me. Grant me the desire to pursue my job with excellence, energy, and edification. I want to do my best to serve those you have given to my care. I want to be uplifting and not hinder their success.*

## 24
# ENEMY MINE

## THE RIGHT WORDS

*Be self-controlled and alert. Your enemy the devil prowls around
like a roaring lion looking for someone to devour. Resist him,
standing firm in the faith, because you know that your brothers
throughout the world are undergoing the same kind of sufferings.*

1 PETER 5:8–9

## SPOKEN AT THE RIGHT TIME

The roaring lioness is on the prowl. She looks for the weak
and the stragglers to devour. Satan's method is the same.
Sometimes our cares, concerns, and challenges cause us to
separate ourselves from the fellowship of other believers and
ultimately from God's protection. "These are burdensome,
and often very sinful, when they arise from unbelief and dis-
trust, when they torture and distract the mind, unfit us for
duties, and hinder our delight in the service of God."[1]

We must cast our cares upon God and leave every event at the foot of the cross. We can believe that God's will and counsel are right and be at peace with this truth. We too often forget this and worry ourselves to the point of ineffectiveness. Then we find ourselves vulnerable to attack.

We can stand firm and be reminded that our brothers and sisters in Christ experience the same turmoil. We can all experience God's deliverance and peace.

## BRING UNDERSTANDING AND PEACE

One of the ways the Enemy works is to make us feel like we are completely alone in our trials and struggles—that no one else could possibly understand what we are going through. When we feel alone, we tend to isolate ourselves even further and find ourselves truly alone. Teachers are good at isolating themselves.

Teachers have families and responsibilities outside the classroom that affect how we do our jobs. Usually we keep our cares to ourselves and under wraps. The thought of looking weak is unacceptable and frightening. In this age of accountability no teacher wants a hint of inability or disability.

When I was pregnant with our first child my colleagues and students were thrilled for me. It was such a joy to share this blessed event with them month by month. But then at twenty weeks I lost our baby girl—and my ability to share my personal life with my school community. I retreated into myself and was perceived as unapproachable by many. It was self-protection in an attempt to heal—like a Band-Aid to a wound. But wounds need air to speed the healing, and I wasn't coming up for air.

A couple of teachers tried to reach out to me while I convalesced. One brought a beautiful book—*Sonnets From the Portuguese* by Elizabeth Barrett Browning—and another came just to sit with me. I wanted neither. I wanted to be alone. My students tried to reach out to me and I pushed them away, vowing never to allow myself to become attached again. Help was offered; I just wasn't taking it.

We all have things in our lives that incapacitate us for a time. Why we think we must handle them by ourselves is a mystery to me, but so common. Even if we feel we aren't teaching well, the tendency is to pull away in silence. The fear of revelation is exactly what the Enemy wants. He wants to separate you from those who have been placed in your life to help you and point you to the source of all hope. Don't let him have that power!

I may not have allowed those teachers to help me, but to this day I thank God for their attempts to offer help. They planted seeds that have grown into a God-given compassion that I can give to others.

## ONE HEART AT A TIME

You are not alone! The adage "United we stand, divided
we fall" is true even in a biblical sense. Stand tall with your
brothers and sisters in Christ. Don't be tempted to pull
away and separate yourself to grieve over your concerns.
Do not give the Enemy a foothold in your life!

## PRAYER

*Heavenly Father, I am so anxious about what will
happen. I fear for my future, agonize over the present,
and have great regret over the past. I know you see
everything from the beginning to the end of my days. Help
me now to rest in your sovereignty and rely on the hope of
your salvation. You alone are holy. You alone are the
Lord. I know I do not have to be alone in this.*

# 25

# £IKE MANNA FROM HEAVEN

## THE RIGHT WORDS

*The Lord said to Moses, "I have heard the grumbling of the Israelites. Tell them, 'At twilight you will eat meat, and in the morning you will be filled with bread. Then you will know that I am the Lord your God.'"*

EXODUS 16:11–12

## SPOKEN AT THE RIGHT TIME

D o you know that the Lord is *your* God? He is not only the God of the Israelites, He is yours! Sometimes we forget that and He has to remind us. When we begin to fret, we must remember that God hears all our complaints. God promises a speedy and constant supply of grace. Why do we forget so quickly His faithfulness?

It is a beautiful thing that even while they whined and complained, God fed the Israelites. And not just with any food. He gave them the sweetest manna and best meat. God goes above and beyond the call of duty for us every day. It is more than enough!

## BRING UNDERSTANDING AND PEACE

I was so grateful to have a job, but I knew by the end of the first week of school that it was a mistake. The stress level in our home rose to unrivaled proportions. My children were anxious. My husband was frustrated. And I was beside myself with guilt. I should have stayed home. I thought things would improve for us financially if I went back to teaching, but at what cost?

Everyone at my school knew I was unhappy. Even the parents of my students knew. How could they not? I complained to anyone who would listen. I knew this job was God's providence for us, but it had such a negative effect on my home life that it was hard to see His provision from here.

I signed a year-long contract, and I wasn't about to break it. I couldn't see how I was going to survive this school year. I used up all my sick days in the first six weeks because my younger son was sick more often than not. Somehow our financial situation became worse and our pile of debt grew into a mountain. The challenges drove me to despair, and I felt trapped as in a well, unable to reach the sunlight.

*How do I do this, Lord?* I cried. *How am I supposed to get through this week, let alone this school year?*

God's provision for us didn't end with my getting a job. He gave me the grace each and every morning to sustain me. It was new every day! But just as the Israelites were given manna from heaven during their wanderings in the desert, and had to gather it for themselves, so I had to gather God's grace each morning. I can't believe I wasted so much time in the desert complaining when I could have had sweet manna to eat and known that it was from God.

That year I did wander in a desert. It may have been the job God provided for our needs, but my attitude of discontent tarnished the gift. God is patient. He waited while I grumbled, but at the same time He fed me the sweet bread of His grace. It didn't change how often my son got sick or the amount of takeout we ordered instead of preparing home-cooked meals. But the promise of new grace every morning became enough for me to get through that most stressful school year—one day at a time.

## ONE HEART AT A TIME

Do you wonder if you'll make it through this school year?
Does the thought of six or nine more months of teaching
give you a panic attack? Don't worry about tomorrow.
God's grace is for today! Gather it up
and savor its sweetness.

## PRAYER

*My God, I praise you for your faithfulness in my life,
especially when I am not faithful at all. You provide for
all that I need and more. You will never leave or forsake
me. You are my God and I am yours! Blessed be the name
of the Lord.*

Sometimes the days and weeks of a school year blur together. It's hard to see progress, let alone success. Yet there are daily victories, though they may be small. Think back over the past week and find those small victories. Thank God for them now. List them as a reminder of God's faithfulness.

### INTO YOUR HANDS, LORD . . .

*Pray for*

_____

_____

_____

_____

_____

*For we are His workmanship, created in Christ Jesus for good works, which God prepared beforehand that we should walk in them.*
EPHESIANS 2:10 NKJV

# 26

# WHEN THE THRILL IS GONE

## THE RIGHT WORDS

*Arm yourselves also with the same attitude [as Christ].* . . .
*[Do] not live the rest of [your] earthly life for . . .
human desires, but rather for the will of God.*

1 PETER 4:1–2

## SPOKEN AT THE RIGHT TIME

D ying, He destroyed our sin. Rising, He restored our life.
That was what Christ did and why He did it. He did it
out of love and to do the will of the Father. Peter exhorts us
to go forth with the same attitude, living our lives to share
God's love and to do His will. In arming ourselves, we take
the time to prepare ourselves for the daily battle and use what

is at our disposal—prayer and the Word of God.

Not my will, but yours be done, Lord!

## BRING UNDERSTANDING AND PEACE

I was always on the hunt for a new or better way to teach so that I could reach as many of my students as possible. I looked for ways to infuse excitement and enthusiasm into my teaching, not only to motivate my students but to motivate myself. I guess you could call me a *thrill-seeker teacher*.

I didn't roll my eyes at the prospect of another in-service workshop or a motivational speaker. I desperately wanted to hold on to that idealistic exhilaration that brand-new teachers feel. I was afraid of falling into the mundane day to day survival mode so many veteran teachers seemed to display.

I wanted what felt good to last—but it can't and, truth be told, it shouldn't. We rely entirely too much on our human senses. We judge people and situations by our feelings about them. My husband hates walking into schools because they have a smell that reminds him of never feeling quite good enough and disappointing his teachers and parents. The sights, smells, and sounds of a school bring up bad feelings for him, so he avoids it. I personally enjoy the mix of cleaning fluid, chalk dust (or dry erase markers), and meat loaf surprise wafting through the overdue-to-be-cleaned ventilation system. I love the sound of the bell and the look of recently polished linoleum floors. They bring back wonderful memories for me, so they attract me.

We are no longer born of the flesh, but of the Spirit. We should not depend on the senses of the flesh to discern a particular situation or to help us make a choice. The thrill may be gone from your first days in the classroom. That's okay. It's a part of the natural cycle of teaching. Don't depend upon warm fuzzies to get you through. Depend on the Spirit instead. We are called to put to death our old ways and seek to live by the Spirit. Empty yourself of your own sensory perceptions and be filled with the attitude of Christ. It's the only real, lasting way to persevere.

## ONE HEART AT A TIME

God's provision for you may indeed be a motivational speaker or a new technique. But don't go in search of a quick fix. Learn how to be still and rest in the steadiness of God's Spirit instead.

## PRAYER

*Lord, let me follow the model your Son left for me—to do your will out of a desire to serve. Help me to be still, know that you are God, and immerse myself in your Word so that I will indeed be armed with the attitude of Christ.*

# 27

# ℐENDER MERCIES

## THE RIGHT WORDS

*Speak and act as those who are going to be judged by the law that gives freedom, because judgment without mercy will be shown to anyone who has not been merciful. Mercy triumphs over judgment!*

JAMES 2:12–13

## SPOKEN AT THE RIGHT TIME

God is the just Judge. His judgment is tempered by His mercy. Those of us in Christ may serve Him without slavish fear. Our own poor choices and offenses are the only things that restrain us from experiencing God's glory and peace in our lives. We should be condemned on that final day, and yet He will show mercy instead.

For whom much is given, much is expected. Students will receive natural consequences for their transgressions, but we must judge their deeds with mercy. We must copy God's mercy in our own conduct toward others.

## BRING UNDERSTANDING AND PEACE

There are daily challenges to our authority as teachers. Students aren't always compliant, willing learners. Defiance rears its ugly head and before you know it you have a power struggle on your hands. There was a time when I believed it was most important that I "win" at all cost. But sometimes the cost is too high—the spirit of a child in my care.

Students make poor choices. They choose to go their own way and disregard our instruction. They often fail as a result of following their own will. We can use our power as the authority in their lives to give life, or we can use it to humble and sometimes humiliate students. I remember teachers in my life who believed that intimidation was the best way to control a class. Fear was indeed a motivator to me as a young student, but when I entered high school I felt sorry for the teachers who ran their classes that way. They obviously didn't think they could keep order any other way.

When I became a teacher, I knew that I'd have to deal with difficult students, but I wanted to do it in a way that didn't crush their spirits. There would be plenty of opportunities to deliver judgment, but fewer chances to apply mercy.

Sometimes students are just plain foolish, and harsh judgment is not the way to go. They will still experience natural consequences, but the life-giving result of your mercy as their teacher is quite powerful.

## ONE HEART AT A TIME

Within our care our students become our children. Fathers are instructed not to exasperate their children. We would do well to follow this command as well. Be fair. Be consistent. Be merciful. Students need structure, but they need relationship too. Balance your judgment with mercy and you will give them just what they need.

### PRAYER

*My God, you are the only just Judge. Every day I have an opportunity to administer justice, but I realize now that it is also a chance for me to extend mercy! I want to follow your model, so that in time my students will follow mine.*

# 28

# ᴀLL FOR ONE AND ONE FOR ALL

## THE RIGHT WORDS

*As you sent me into the world, so I sent them into the world. And
I consecrate myself for them, so that they may also be consecrated
in truth. I pray not only for them, but also for those who will
believe in me through their word, so that they may all be one, as
you, Father, are in me and I in you, that they also may be in us,
that the world may believe that you sent me . . .
and that you loved them even as you loved me.*

JOHN 17:18–21, 23 NAB

## SPOKEN AT THE RIGHT TIME

It's all connected—we are set apart, and Christ was set
apart. Christ prays for us, and we pray for others. This is
all for one purpose—to be one with the Father, the Son, and

the Holy Spirit as they are one. What a picture! It is not for ourselves that we love one another, but so that the world will see that love in us and believe in the God that sent us into the world. We are part of an incredibly big purpose. How humbling that fact is for each and every one of us.

## BRING UNDERSTANDING AND PEACE

I love learning, and as a teacher I always wanted my students to love learning as well. I knew the love of learning was a fire that when ignited could take them far beyond their dreams. Yet as educators one of our greatest challenges is student motivation. It didn't matter if I taught highly gifted students or struggling learning-disabled students, or if I substituted in a regular classroom—I always asked the same question: *Lord, how do I get into their hearts? Because it's the only way they will understand.*

All the studying I did to prepare for my vocation didn't teach me how to reach into the hearts of my students. I knew strategies and approaches but not the heart issues that are necessary for change and growth. Oh, how I wanted my students to grow!

Those of us who are Christian teachers are one. Christ prays for us that through our words others may come to Him and be one with us. I want my students to see Christ through me. I want them to have a hunger to learn, but I also want them to know truth. Even in a public school, I can speak God's truth without quoting chapter and verse. I am not handicapped from doing so. My decisions can be biblically based. My attitudes can be a reflection of Christ's. My actions should mimic those of Christ while He was on this earth. I can do all this and teach language arts. I can do all this and help a struggling student. I can do all this through Christ who strengthens me. And in doing so, I can attract more to the kingdom where we become one.

## ONE HEART AT A TIME

Why do we do what we do? It cannot be for us alone. It cannot be to please ourselves. Education is about relationship. Build a better relationship and you help build a better student and eventually build up the body of Christ.

### PRAYER

*Lord, I want to do all that I do in your name. In the name of the Father, Son, and Holy Spirit I serve you here on earth. Let all that I do and all that I say bring glory to your name and ultimately bring others to yourself. Help me to be constantly connected to you so that I can offer connection to those around me.*

# 29

# $\mathcal{T}$HE PURSUIT OF HOLINESS

## THE RIGHT WORDS

*Therefore, strengthen your feeble arms and weak knees. "Make level paths for your feet," so that the lame may not be disabled, but rather healed. Make every effort to live in peace with all men and to be holy; without holiness no one will see the Lord. See to it that no one misses the grace of God and that no bitter root grows up to cause trouble and defile many.*

HEBREWS 12:12–15

## SPOKEN AT THE RIGHT TIME

There will be times when we are afflicted with something that gets in the way of our joyous service to the Lord. A physical ailment, chronic illness, or injury may color our lives with disappointment, discouragement, and even despair.

In these verses from Hebrews, the author encourages us to do whatever it takes to strengthen ourselves even in our weaknesses so that only holiness will be center stage and not our discouragement or disability. We don't want someone to follow our lead to God because they feel sorry for us but because they are attracted to someone who exhibits holiness even while battling an affliction.

## BRING UNDERSTANDING AND PEACE

Even a Teacher of the Year™ is not perfect. We all have weaknesses and things about ourselves and our teaching that need improvement. Those teachers who desire to improve their craft willingly enroll in workshops and extra classes to discover how they might improve. But we can be the most engaging, exciting, and educated teachers and not be holy.

My walk of faith is always watched carefully by my students and my colleagues, whether I realize it or not. It is a matter of *show-and-tell*. I remember loving show-and-tell as a child, as a teacher, and then as a parent. I giggled in anticipation of my own son carrying his precious treasure cupped in his tiny hands to kindergarten. The kids in his class couldn't wait to see what he brought. They were much more interested in what he brought to show than what he had to say. The power was in the show!

Holiness is cultivated in us by paying attention to Christ's holiness while He walked this earth in human form. It was a matter of what He did, and not only what He said, that transformed lives. My pursuit of holiness doesn't only affect me— it is not for my own sake. My students will learn what holiness looks like, acts like, and speaks like by watching me do what I do each and every day. It is for their sake that I pursue holiness.

Even within a public school, I can pursue holiness. The stakes are high. If I don't, then I may become a hindrance to others who would come to Christ. As we teach children, we need to become painfully aware of Christ's desire that they come to Him. I can be the bridge. It is my choice.

## ONE HEART AT A TIME

Holiness is a choice. There may be a parent or a child who
is a thorn in our side, but we can still be holy. We may
have personal problems at home, but we can still be holy.
We may battle an illness, but we can still be holy.
We can be holy because Christ is holy!

## PRAYER

*Lord, you are holy indeed—the fountain of all holiness. Let me come to you when I am weary or brokenhearted and drink from your well of living water. Restore my soul so that I may be a source of your holiness to those you put in my path.*

# 30
# *C*OPYCAT

## THE RIGHT WORDS

*Be imitators of God, therefore, as dearly loved children and live a*
*life of love, just as Christ loved us and gave himself up for*
*us as a fragrant offering and sacrifice to God.*

EPHESIANS 5:1–2

## SPOKEN AT THE RIGHT TIME

Because God, for Christ's sake, has forgiven us, we are to
be followers and imitators of God. We can pattern ourselves especially after His love and pardoning goodness. We
love Him and desire to grow up to be just like Him. Because
of Christ's sacrifice, we can stand before a holy God as a sweet
aroma to Him. The stench of our sins is extinguished and He
recognizes us as one of His own. We must consider this truth
as we conduct ourselves each and every day.

## BRING UNDERSTANDING AND PEACE

I've never been comfortable praying aloud in front of others. Somehow I don't feel as eloquent as those who pray around me. I wonder if God hears my not-so-perfect cries. There have been times when I felt as if I were auditioning for the prayer team. I've never made any team I've tried out for.

Even within the prayer circle we had at our school, I would stand there, palms sweaty, anxious about how to open my mouth without trembling. I guess I'm not cut out for praying in public. And I finally realized that there wasn't anything wrong with that.

Jesus took time daily to pray, and He always went away to do it. It soothes me to know that I'm not a failure for preferring to pray alone. I may not always be silent when I pray—far from it! Countless times my cries have been loud enough to worry my neighbors.

Within our schools we have opportunities daily to be imitators of Christ. As we meet together in prayer, we can respect each individual's call to pray. There are no rules except those which will help conform us to His image. There may be teachers in your midst who would pray with you if they knew it wasn't a requirement to pray aloud. We want to be imitators, not intimidators.

## ONE HEART AT A TIME

We were made in God's image. Our ultimate goal is to resemble Him in as many ways as possible. The most powerful way is in the way that we love. His love overcomes any boundaries that exist in our schools and with our colleagues. Our differences only create a beautiful tapestry that is of God's making. Let it cover us all when we pray, when we love, and when we serve one another.

### PRAYER

*Lord Jesus, day by day, week by week I am being transformed from my selfish image to your selfless image. Hasten my transformation so that I may do the work you've prepared for me, conscious that I am your hands and feet here on earth.*

In the book of Genesis we're told that Cain and Abel each brought an offering to the Lord from the labors they were called to do. Abel's offering was accepted but Cain's was not. Cain became angry and defensive. God encouraged him to seek what was right and not let sin claim him, but Cain refused to hear it. We all know what happened next. In Hebrews 11:4 Abel is described as making his offering by faith.

As teachers responding to a call, we can do our job as a sacrificial offering to God. It doesn't matter where we teach, how much money we earn, how well our students behave, or how involved their parents are. What matters is that we offer up our work to the Lord in faith. Do we do it with His glory in mind and to the best of the ability He gave us? Or do we do the bare minimum to get by in our own strength? Pray this weekend that God will reveal the motives of your heart. Seek forgiveness for any motives that are not pleasing in His sight. Pray that your sacrifice will be acceptable to God as you work each day for His children.

### INTO YOUR HANDS, LORD . . .

*Pray for*

_____

_____

*For the grace of God that brings salvation has appeared to all men, teaching us that, denying ungodliness and worldly lusts, we should live soberly, righteously, and godly, in this present world.*

Titus 2:11–12 NKJV

# 31
# PASS IT ON

## THE RIGHT WORDS

*I will sing of the Lord's great love forever; with my mouth I will make your faithfulness known through all generations. I will declare that your love stands firm forever, that you established your faithfulness in heaven itself.*

PSALM 89:1–2

## SPOKEN AT THE RIGHT TIME

Teachers are usually great talkers. We open our mouths and dispense knowledge. And yet pursuing knowledge is a vain pursuit. We may be paired with these students as part of their eventual equipping to serve in the kingdom of God. Our part is not the end but the beginning. If they learn anything from us, let it be how to give glory and honor to God the Almighty Father. If we cannot do it with our words, let us do it with our actions.

## BRING UNDERSTANDING AND PEACE

The first year I taught a gifted education class I began in the middle of the semester. I hit the ground running, and for the remainder of the year I felt like I'd never catch up. There were many parents that year who were skeptical of my position, and they spent their time undermining me to both my principal and their children. They didn't even know me, yet they judged me.

That same year I lost our first child in utero, and the words of my critics finally stopped. What followed was painful silence. Until one day a parent came to see me with a gift. It was a baby book.

"This is for when you have your next child," she said as if she could predict the future.

"Thank you, but I don't think I'll get pregnant again any time soon," I said. I didn't want to offend her, but this gift was breaking my heart.

"God is faithful," she said. "Even when we're not or don't believe He is. Accept this by faith."

I knew inside she was talking about more than the book. Her words blessed me. Her words brought some healing. But mostly, her words proclaimed God's faithfulness in a way that has affected me profoundly ever since.

I wanted to be able to do that for my students. There were days when it was difficult to find any words of blessing to say to them, but I made it my mission to find some. What if my words were the ones that stuck with a student for his whole life? What he thought about school would someday be passed on to his children. I wanted to pass on God's faithfulness, not my failings.

## ONE HEART AT A TIME

Teachers use their words to change lives. We make known truths about a variety of subjects. We have the power to encourage and sometimes discourage a child. We can lead with our words in a way that affects students for the rest of their lives.

## PRAYER

*Lord, your Word is truth! My words can be faulty or painful or not worth listening to. Please help me choose my words and guide my tongue. Help me to discern the occasion so that I know when to speak and when to be quiet. When I am quiet and still before you I long to hear your words.*

## 32
# WHO IS MY NEIGHBOR, LORD?

## THE RIGHT WORDS

*He answered: "Love the Lord your God with all your heart and with all your soul and with all your strength and with all your mind"; and, "Love your neighbor as yourself." . . . "And who is my neighbor?" . . . "Which of these three do you think was a neighbor to the man who fell into the hands of robbers?" The expert in the law replied, "The one who had mercy on him." Jesus told him, "Go and do likewise."*

LUKE 10:27, 29, 36–37

## SPOKEN AT THE RIGHT TIME

Even those of us who don't eat right or exercise or get enough sleep still treat ourselves better than we treat others. We look out for number one! We probably spend more time and energy on ourselves than anyone else. What if we turned that energy and effort around to meet the needs of someone else? Teachers are great at caring for the children in their classrooms, but we're not very good at observing, identifying, and meeting the needs of our colleagues. Yet God commands us to show mercy and help to meet the needs of our neighbors.

Behind the closed classroom doors at many schools are teachers who are in need but who live and work in quiet desperation. Can we reach outside of ourselves enough to touch the shoulder of our neighbor and be the means God chooses to meet their need?

## BRING UNDERSTANDING AND PEACE

Special education teachers are the stepchildren of education. That was never more painfully obvious to me than during my very first teaching assignment.

The portable classroom I shared with another special education teacher reeked of its previous function—the custodian's storage room. The custodian had a new room in the main building. We were relegated to this fifteen-year-old portable classroom far from the main building, a room that wasn't even safe during the severe storms we saw on Florida's Gulf Coast. No one even knew we were out there. I saw it on their faces when I'd enter the teacher's lunchroom. They had no idea who I was or what I taught.

The division between "regular" classroom teachers and special education teachers grew steadily, and by the end of my first year of teaching I accepted the fact that it would always be "us against them." How sad.

I learned from the example other special education teachers set for me: If there was a problem I needed to handle it myself. I knew that if I needed additional materials or supplies, it was up to me to find them on my own time and with my own money. I also knew that if any of my students caused any trouble, the administration would have no mercy on them. I became self-protective and isolated myself by eating in my classroom instead of the lunchroom. Somehow it felt safer.

Until the day my portable classroom was violently vandalized. I lost everything. The five computers I got as a result of a grant, the art supplies that were donated to us from an area fine arts center, and the furniture my husband's company donated were all irreparably damaged. I sat on the floor and cried in despair.

I know what it feels like to be the Samaritan. Fortunately, what it has done is cultivate a sense of mercy in me for others who feel left out and alone. But at some schools isolation is the norm. Can we reach out to our neighbors? Can we at least peek into the rooms of those in our hallway and say hello?

## ONE HEART AT A TIME

While we were still sinners, the blessed Jesus had compassion on us. Jesus loved us and gave His life for us while we were still His enemies; and having shown us mercy, He bids us to go and do likewise. It is the duty of us all according to our ability to comfort, help, and relieve those in our midst who are in distress.

## PRAYER

*Lord, there are so many needs around me. Everyone seems to want a piece of me! How can I relieve the pain I see? How can I, by myself, make a difference? There are those that I avoid because of their nature or attitude or neediness. Help me to reach out to them instead of hiding behind my own closed door. Give me what I need so that I may meet the needs of those you have given to me.*

# 33

# TRUE HOPE

## THE RIGHT WORDS

*Hope deferred makes a heart sick, but a longing
fulfilled is a tree of life.*

PROVERBS 13:12

## SPOKEN AT THE RIGHT TIME

Every person on this planet is looking for hope. We just
happen to be looking for it in all the wrong places. When
what we hope for never comes to pass, it makes us sick.
Believers and non-believers alike suffer from anxiety, addic-
tions, and behaviors that alienate them from the healing
power of God's grace.

When a hope that is within us is finally fulfilled, it brings
life and more hope. But the world is bound to disappoint us,
and it is foolish to put our hopes in the things of this world.
God is the only one who will never let us down. He will never

leave or forsake us! Our true hope lies in the salvation Christ has already secured for us. It is a done deal. The hope of eternal life is upon us—right here and right now.

## BRING UNDERSTANDING AND PEACE

What attracts us to teaching? Especially with all the bad press, it still amazes me that people feel an inexplicable pull to the classroom. Choosing to enroll as an education major when I went off to college was met by a barrage of criticism from many of my contemporaries and even some of my elders.

"Teaching isn't respected; why do it?"

"There's no money in it."

"Taking care of other people's children? That sounds frustrating."

It was easy for me to dismiss their naysaying. I wanted to teach. That's all there was to it. I had hope that I could make a difference. I couldn't wait to see if I actually could.

Five years later the naysayers' words crept again into my tired brain.

*I rarely see progress. Some of these kids just aren't going to make it. No matter what I do some of them still fail. Maybe it's time to get out.*

My hope was bound up in the success of my students. I taught severely learning-disabled students at the time, and hope was difficult to find. If I were going to remain I needed to put my hope in something and someone who wouldn't fail.

So often we lose hope because it is misplaced in the first place. Place your hope in Jesus Christ and what He did to reconcile us to himself, and you will learn to lean on that hope when faced with insurmountable odds.

## ONE HEART AT A TIME

We have an abundance of reasons to be discouraged in the job of teaching. We are all sinners and will disappoint one another. It's a fact of life here on earth. Choose instead to place your hope in the One who has already gained the victory over your problems with difficult students, expectations of parents, frustrating colleagues, and an often disinterested society. Your hope is in Him alone!

### PRAYER

*Heavenly Father, I believe you are who you say you are. I trust in your faithfulness. I look forward to living in your presence in heaven. Help me to live now in the hope of that day.*

# 34
# $\mathcal{D}$O AS I DO

## THE RIGHT WORDS

*After that, he poured water into a basin and began to wash his disciples' feet, drying them with the towel that was wrapped around him. He came to Simon Peter, who said to him, "Lord, are you going to wash my feet?" Jesus replied, "You do not realize now what I am doing, but later you will understand."*

JOHN 13:5–7

## SPOKEN AT THE RIGHT TIME

We don't always see at the moment the reason for our present circumstances. Clarity tends to come in hindsight. Our students won't know the importance of the lessons we taught them. Our own children won't know that we were "right" until they are much older. And sometimes an act of selfless kindness seems unnecessary and even embarrassing.

Jesus not only washed the disciples' feet to illustrate a spiritual washing, He took the place of the least among them and met their needs. He showed them how to serve others.

## BRING UNDERSTANDING AND PEACE

P ositions of leadership within schools are difficult if not at times impossible. Your desire to do good and make a difference in the lives of children and teachers can consume you until you realize one day that your hands are tied and you can't make the *big* changes. Keeping teachers motivated and spurring them on to do good works with their students is a constant challenge. The best education leaders are those whose primary desire is to serve. I had one such principal.

Sue Baley taught in the classroom for more than fifteen years before becoming a principal. She believed in practicing what she preached, so when one of her teachers was in need, she was the one who came to her aid—she didn't delegate. There were times when a teacher went home sick or had to leave unexpectedly because of a family emergency. Sue Baley stepped in as teacher without hesitation. The day she did it for me was a gift I will never forget.

I was light-headed from the moment I awoke that day, but I went to school anyway. I had already exhausted my allotted sick days due to my difficult pregnancy and couldn't afford not to work. But just before third period I couldn't even stand up. My teaching partner called my husband who came to take me to the doctor. Mrs. Baley sat with me until he showed up. She made me comfortable on the old leather couch in the teachers' lounge and babied me the way my own mother had when I was a child. She was selfless and attentive and I was amazed. Her walkie-talkie squawked the message that the office still hadn't found anyone to cover my classes. She told them she had it under control.

That day Mrs. Baley took my place with twenty-five challenging learning-disabled seventh graders—a group for which she wasn't trained. I felt badly for her because I knew how difficult my students were, and that fact alone kept many a substitute away! I tried to steady myself and rose to stop her from taking my class.

She smiled sweetly at my protests and eased me back onto the couch. "It's why I'm here," she said.

I've carried her attitude of service with me ever since. If there is a way I can ease another teacher's burden or hold her up in the midst of trial, I will. It's why I'm here.

## ONE HEART AT A TIME

Those you serve don't have to understand why you do
what you do for them. You don't have to explain yourself.
Just serve them in the most humble way and someday
they will know why. Show them how to do it! You
may be the only one in their life who does.

### PRAYER

*Lord, help me to remember that I am a part of your body. I want to be your hands, your feet, your eyes—to see with compassion, to do good, and to bless others with your grace.*

# 35
# 𝒯RUTH BE TOLD

## THE RIGHT WORDS

*Therefore each of you must put off falsehood and speak truthfully
to his neighbor, for we are all members of one body. In your anger
do not sin. Do not let the sun go down while you are still angry,
and do not give the devil a foothold. . . . Do not let any
unwholesome talk come out of your mouths, but only what is
helpful for building others up according to their needs,
that it may benefit those who listen.*

EPHESIANS 4:25–27, 29

## SPOKEN AT THE RIGHT TIME

We are given specific guidelines for how we should live. What we do not only affects our own life but the lives of those who watch and listen to what we do and say. The children we teach may not always listen, but they hear every word we say. Their parents may not always see us, but they watch every move we make.

We must take heed of everything contrary to truth. Don't flatter or deceive others into thinking that things are better than they are. God's people are those who will not lie, who dare not lie, who hate lying. If there is an opportunity or need to express displeasure at what is wrong, and to reprove, do so without sinning. Our students and their parents will mirror what they see in us.

## BRING UNDERSTANDING AND PEACE

The conference didn't go as well as expected. Julie turned from my sister in Christ into a ferocious mother bear protecting her less-than-perfect cub. I backtracked quickly, trying to figure out what I had said to set her off. "Danny has trouble turning in assignments on time," was all I remembered saying.

This was a side of Julie I'd never seen before. We went to the same church and had attended the same Bible study. Initially she was thrilled that Danny was in my class, but now it was obvious she regretted the fact.

The rest of the conference was unproductive and a waste of time. Julie was hurt, and I didn't know what to say or do to make it better. She left in a huff, and I sat in my classroom dumbfounded. Now what? With absolutely no intention, I'd alienated a parent, a friend, and a fellow believer. I waited three weeks hoping I'd hear from her, but the icy silence prevailed.

Danny began to turn in his work on time, but his happy-go-lucky ten-year-old demeanor changed; he became a guarded, compliant fifth-grader. On the outside I got what I wanted—Danny took his schoolwork seriously—but somehow it felt like a hollow victory.

I knew I hadn't said anything wrong. I knew Julie reacted in a way I couldn't explain. I knew it was her problem and not mine. But I'd hurt her nevertheless.

I called Julie and made peace.

## ONE HEART AT A TIME

A parent/teacher conference is an opportunity first to let parents get to know us and second to communicate truth. But we must be on our guard to speak the truth in love, and if we cannot do so, we should be silent.

## PRAYER

*Lord, just as you came in peace, let my realm of influence be one of peace as well. Let my speech be free from untruth and let it be a welcome salve on a wounded soul. Let me begin each conference in a way that says, "Peace be with you."*

Sometimes it's not enough to "take it one step at a time" or just "put one foot in front of the other." Sometimes we need to take a step back. We need a retreat. We usually know we need a retreat when it is almost too late. We're overwhelmed, overworked, and underappreciated. No one else is going to tell you to stop, book you at a tranquil bed and breakfast, and serve your every need. You're going to have to take that step back—that retreat—by yourself.

It might mean dropping a few activities in and out of school. It might mean taking a well deserved personal day. It might mean an actual sabbatical or leave of absence. Whatever it means for you, you have to take control of it and enter into God's rest—something He created for our good and His glory.

If at this very moment you can't even fathom what rest looks like in your life, pray for wisdom and opportunity. Meditate on what it means to rest in the Lord—to abide in Him. God is waiting for you to come so He can give you rest.

## INTO YOUR HANDS, LORD . . .

*Pray for*

_____

_____

*And he said unto them, "Come ye yourselves apart into a desert place, and rest a while": for there were many coming and going, and they had no leisure so much as to eat. And they departed into a desert place by ship privately.*
MARK 6:31–32 KJV

# 36
# SING FROM THE MOUNTAINTOPS

## THE RIGHT WORDS

*My heart is steadfast, God; my heart is steadfast. I will sing and chant praise. Awake my soul; awake, lyre and harp! I will wake the dawn. I will praise you among the peoples, Lord; I will chant your praise among the nations. For your love towers to the heavens; your faithfulness, to the skies. Appear on high over the heavens, God; may your glory appear above all the earth. Help with your right hand and answer us that your loved ones may escape.*

PSALM 108:1–7 NAB

## SPOKEN AT THE RIGHT TIME

G od has gifted us with the ability to devise songs, chants, and prayers of worship and praise. Whatever it is and whatever it takes to proclaim His glory is what we should do! Psalms are a wonderful way to meditate on the goodness of God, so that when our hearts are troubled we can go to a source of praise and thanksgiving to refocus our prayers.

## BRING UNDERSTANDING AND PEACE

Teaching in a public school is not conducive to public prayer or praise of our Lord. But that doesn't mean we can't praise him with silent fervency.

Songs of worship and praise have always been my preferred way of praise. Songs can be like chants, communicating over and over again the mercy, faithfulness, love, or forgiveness of God. They help me focus on what is true, especially during times of extreme trial or persecution. But music is not possible during the school day.

I found a prayer that outlined all I needed as a teacher and took me to the foot of God's throne to meet those needs. The prayer of St. Francis, for me, has been a gentle reminder of what I should do in the face of disobedient students, challenging parents, and frustrating colleagues. I memorized it so that I could fill my mind with God's way and not my own. Memorizing favorite Scripture passages also helps focus us on God's truth.

Silently you can enter into His rest with praise and supplication.

The Prayer of St. Francis

Lord, make me an instrument of Thy peace.
Where there is hatred, let me sow love;
where there is injury, pardon;
where there is doubt, faith;
where there is despair, hope;
where there is darkness, light;
And where there is sadness, joy.
O Divine Master,
grant that I may not so much seek
to be consoled as to console;
to be understood as to understand;
to be loved as to love;
for it is in giving that we receive;
it is in pardoning that we are pardoned,
and it is in dying that we are born to eternal life.

## ONE HEART AT A TIME

We live in a distracting world. We need tools to help us
focus on the things above—on God's goodness, on His
truths, and on His kingdom. Look for tangible ways to
stop, bow, and give praise to our Father in heaven.

## PRAYER

*Lord, God, Heavenly King, Almighty God and Father! I worship you. I give you thanks. I praise you for your glory! Let me take the time each day to proclaim your goodness in the gates. Let me lift my voice in praise to the glory of your name!*

# 37

# ℳame Above All Names

## THE RIGHT WORDS

*For I am already being poured out like a drink offering, and the time has come for my departure. I have fought the good fight, I have finished the race, I have kept the faith. Now there is in store for me the crown of righteousness, which the Lord, the righteous Judge, will award to me on that day—and not only to me, but also to all who have longed for his appearing.*

2 TIMOTHY 4:6–8

## SPOKEN AT THE RIGHT TIME

Many of us measure our days by whether we were recognized for doing good. There is a fine line between doing good even in the midst of a trial and being a "martyr." Those who tend toward the dramatic, struggle with this distinction more than others. Our goal should be that at the time our life here ends we will have peace that we fought the good fight and finished the race whether it was noted by others or not.

There is a reward awaiting us. The crown of righteousness is real, and it will be awarded to us by the King of Glory! Remember that it is really His righteousness lived out in us that is being identified. That's why on that day we will cast our crowns at His feet in final recognition.

## BRING UNDERSTANDING AND PEACE

I'm certainly not at the end of my life, but I do remember the last time I left the classroom.

You could characterize my teaching career to that point as one of perseverance. I worked tirelessly on behalf of my students who had special needs. It felt like a battle much of the time. My efforts rarely were recognized by those who gave awards or rewards to teachers. There were times when I became discouraged. Couldn't they see how hard I worked? Didn't they know the value of what I had to offer?

It took until I left teaching for a time to realize that looking for praise here on earth was not the motive that was pleasing to God. I spent that last year in humble service, and it was the sweetest year of my teaching career.

God doesn't hold out His crowns like carrots to motivate

us to move toward Him. They are a supernatural result of what we did while on this earth. His name is to be praised above all others, even Teacher of the Year℠!

## ONE HEART AT A TIME

Sometimes it's hard to recognize in our society of winners and losers, superstars and supermodels, heads of state and heads of companies, who is really worthy of our praise. But there is one name worthy above all names. Offer your sacrificial praise to Him.

## PRAYER

*"Jesus, name above all names, Beautiful Savior, glorious Lord; Emmanuel, God is with us, Blessed Redeemer, Living Word."* [1] *Let me make your name known by living out your word in my life. Let me be a signpost of your holiness and a billboard of your faithfulness!*

# 38

# ABOVE AND BEYOND THE CALL OF DUTY

## THE RIGHT WORDS

*And the Word became flesh and dwelt among us.*
JOHN 1:14 NKJV

## SPOKEN AT THE RIGHT TIME

God did more than people expected or deserved. The Jews expected an earthly king to liberate them from the Romans. He sent His Son as our King on earth and in heaven. He died for us so that we might be reconciled to Him. What amazing love and commitment! It was a sacrifice unrivaled in any time or by anyone in any place. He did it with the desire that all would come to peaceful reconciliation with Him, yet we are unworthy, and many do not accept His precious gift.

Sacrificial love takes on many forms. If we are to be mimickers of the Light of the World, we're going to have to make some significant changes.

## BRING UNDERSTANDING AND PEACE

It never ceases to amaze me how teachers in other cultures take their job more seriously than we do in the United States. Teachers in Japan spend hours after school working with students individually and visiting them at their homes. They are revered. Parents depend on them to ensure their child is educated while they also accept their own role in their child's education as their number-one priority.

For a number of years our school had a sister school in Japan. We corresponded with them regularly, and teachers from both schools made the trip to visit each other. We were connected via the Internet, but more often than not we felt worlds apart. I was inspired by their dedication to their students. I came away from the experience determined to pattern my own dedication after theirs.

I taught sixth grade and decided to offer time after school every day (on days I didn't have a meeting) to any student who wanted extra help. I made sure I called every parent once with positive news by the end of the first grading period. I even paid attention to the extracurricular activities my students engaged in and tried to attend their games, recitals, or displays whenever I could. I gave them my home phone number and told them they could call me whenever they wanted to. Believe it or not, no one abused that privilege.

It was the least I could do.

So often we only do what others are willing to do for us first. We don't stick our necks out. We don't go beyond the call of duty. We play it safe. What if God had played it safe? What if He hadn't sent His only Son to be born a man? He did more than was expected, yet it was exactly what we needed to be saved.

ONE HEART AT A TIME

What we do for our students must go beyond the call.
Do more than is expected and it may be exactly what
a child you teach needs in order to be saved.

## PRAYER

*Lord, I can never repay your kindness and willingness to sacrifice yourself for my sake. Make me more aware of what it means to give to my students sacrificially and without thought of repayment. It is my heart's desire to give at least a fraction of the grace you've shown me.*

# 39
# ℳOTHING WASTED

## THE RIGHT WORDS

*Therefore, my dear brothers, stand firm. Let nothing move you.*
*Always give yourselves fully to the work of the Lord, because*
*you know that your labor in the Lord is not in vain.*

1 CORINTHIANS 15:58

## SPOKEN AT THE RIGHT TIME

Many things in this life are bound to distract and even
derail us from the course set before us. It is our duty
to persevere and stay focused on what the Lord has given us
to do. Teaching is full of things that can discourage and disappoint us. But we can be encouraged knowing that if we ask,
God will increase our faith so that we can immerse ourselves
in the work uniquely prepared for our hands.

## BRING UNDERSTANDING AND PEACE

It's so easy to measure our success by how many of our students earn good grades or test scores. The system is set up to reinforce this measure of success and we are indoctrinated to believe it is all that matters.

There have been times when either my own choices or those of my students resulted in not-so-noteworthy grades or scores. There have been students who, no matter how hard I tried, were either not willing or able to rise to the heights I aspired for them. There have even been weeks or months that my personal life, either physically or emotionally, got in the way of my best work. Were those days wasted?

Nothing is wasted with God. Not my hard work or the work of my students. Not my frustration or my turmoil over my own or my students' lackluster performance. Despite the best work I've ever done, some school years not all my students will succeed. Their success is not the measuring stick of my own success.

My success is rooted in the fact that God works through me. His efforts prevail even if mine don't. He sees my students' lives from the beginning to the end. He knows where each choice, each action, and each word will lead in their lives and mine. I'm so glad He's the one in charge and not me. My vision is nearsighted. I can only see what is right in front of me.

## ONE HEART AT A TIME

When hard work, frustrating work, and work that at times
seems pointless is your work to do, bear it with fortitude
and perseverance, for you are only doing the work God
has prepared for your hands, and none of it is wasted.

## PRAYER

*Lord, my frustrations are many and my rewards come few and far between. Is what I do going to make a difference in the life of any child? I am weak and the light in my eyes is fading. Help me, O Lord. Save me from these disturbances. Grant me peace and fortitude so that I may continue on the path you have set before me.*

# 40
# Us AGAINST THEM

## THE RIGHT WORDS

*"As I began to speak, the Holy Spirit came on them as he had
come on us at the beginning. Then I remembered what the Lord
had said: 'John baptized with water, but you will be baptized with
the Holy Spirit.' So if God gave them the same gift as he gave us,
who believed in the Lord Jesus Christ, who was I to think that I
could oppose God?" When they heard this, they had no further
objections and praised God, saying, "So then, God has
granted even the Gentiles repentance unto life."*

ACTS 11:15–18

## SPOKEN AT THE RIGHT TIME

When Peter returned from Antioch having preached the
gospel to the Gentiles there, he described a "second
Pentecost" where the Holy Spirit descended on the Gentile
believers. This was very troubling to the Jewish Christians

who believed that salvation belonged to them alone.

This account and the passages that follow are reminders that as Christians we are one in the body of Christ—no matter our position. We can share in the grace that was freely given and then reach out to extend it to one another.

## BRING UNDERSTANDING AND PEACE

I don't know why, but schools are a place of rivalry and competition, and not just for students. Teachers, too, take sides, belong to cliques, and ultimately cultivate an "us against them" climate in the school. Whether it is teachers versus administrators, elementary versus secondary, men versus women, veterans versus novices, special education versus regular education, sports versus academics, the lines are drawn.

Whether as a student or later as a teacher, I don't think I ever belonged to the group in power. It's tiring to always be trying to justify why you deserve the same treatment, the same budget, the same perks, or the same clout as everyone else. Unity in a school isn't easy to come by and something those outside of education would never believe. It's bad enough that we deal with society as a whole as "them." When we turn on each other, it's doubly sad.

One year the PTA had enough money from a fund-raiser to give each classroom teacher a $200 discretionary gift. We were all incredibly excited and grateful for this windfall in the middle of the school year. Unfortunately, the excitement quickly turned to squabbling as the definition of a "classroom" teacher was put to the test. Special education teachers weren't considered "classroom" teachers, nor were those who taught the "specials" such as art, P.E., music, or dropout prevention.

I couldn't believe that some people didn't believe others deserved this special gift from the parents. We taught the same children. We had the same need. It broke my heart and my spirit. I didn't want the money if it meant further division among the faculty.

Thank goodness we had a wise principal. He spoke out on behalf of all of us, those who were "classroom" teachers and those who were not. The money belonged to all of us and that was how the PTA had intended it. We each received the $200. I still hold that principal in high regard. He didn't do the popular thing, but he did the right thing that day.

## ONE HEART AT A TIME

We have an advocate with the Father: Jesus Christ. Here on
earth we can be an advocate for other believers,
whether they teach as we teach or where we teach.
We are advocates of God's grace.

## PRAYER

*Lord, the lines are already drawn at my school. Help
me to be one who crosses the line or blurs the line so that
we can freely give grace to all those called to your
kingdom.*

The quest for unity seems to get lost in the quest for equity in schools. We focus on the wrong ideal. Equity is not obtainable. Unity can be. The only equality that truly exists is that of our status before God. We were created equal, and with Him there is no preferential treatment. That's where our unity lies—in equality before God.

You can probably make a list of all the things that are unfair about your school—things you don't have that others do. I'm asking you to tear up that list and make another one.

List those in your school, including students and parents, who make unity seem impossible. And remember, you might have to put your own name on that list. If you are having difficulty relating to someone, you are no doubt partially to blame.

Now use the list as your prayer guide. Pray for each one and the circumstances that create disharmony. Pray that God will reveal to you your part in the equation. Pray for unity. God will provide for our needs, but we must make every effort to live peaceably with everyone. It is our charge.

# INTO YOUR HANDS, LORD . . .

*Pray for*

_____

_____

_____

_____

_____

*Two are better than one,*
*Because they have a good reward for their labor.*
*For if they fall, one will lift up his companion.*
*But woe to him who is alone when he falls,*
*For he has no one to help him up.*
*Again, if two lie down together,*
*they will keep warm;*
*But how can one be warm alone?*
*Though one may be overpowered by another,*
*two can withstand him.*
*And a threefold cord is not quickly broken.*

ECCLESIASTES 4:9–12 NKJV

# 41

# THOSE WHO RANT AND RAVE

## THE RIGHT WORDS

*Record my lament; list my tears on your scroll—are*
*they not in your record? . . .*
*Hear me, O God, as I voice my complaint; protect*
*my life from the threat of the enemy.*

PSALM 56:8; 64:1

## SPOKEN AT THE RIGHT TIME

In his distress and fear David comforts himself that God
notices all his grievances and all that breaks his heart. Our
God has a bottle in which he stores the tears of His people.
He observes our hearts with tender concern. David's cry is of
one who knows without a doubt that his God hears him and
protects his life. We can have the same assurance.

## BRING UNDERSTANDING AND PEACE

E very morning before my students arrived I had my quiet time with the Lord. Usually I was reading either a devotional or following a reading plan for the Bible. I only had a few minutes, but I wanted to make sure I spent time in God's Word before my world was invaded.

There were times, however, when I knew before a day even started that it would overwhelm me. Sometimes I just didn't feel well. Other times I felt rejected and alone after a disagreement with my husband before work. And then there was the time I was grieving over the loss of my child. I couldn't focus on the devotional or the reading plan in front of me. So I scanned the Psalms. I can always find a psalm that matches my particular emotion—especially the ones written out of grief or fear or despair. I cried out to the Lord through these psalms and knew that He heard my cry.

Our circumstances don't always inspire praise to God. Sometimes we rant and rave at God because we know that He is the only one who can do anything about our pain. And He does.

More than once I've cried over what seemed like an injustice against me by a parent or a colleague. Many times I gathered my frustration over my students like a mother hen gathers her chicks, and I held on to it tightly. But when I cry out to God about the injustice or the frustration, He records my tears and gives me peace. Sometimes it takes until I am spent and my tears stop. Then I realize that my God is indeed good and the Most High.

## ONE HEART AT A TIME

Whether it is a personal issue, an irate parent, a disobedient child, or a colleague with a sharp tongue, give your complaint to God and leave it there. He can handle it.

## PRAYER

*Hear my cry, O Lord, for I am weary and brokenhearted. Bend your ear to my despair and lead me out from myself into your comfort and peace. You are the source of my joy and to you I give glory and honor!*

# 42

# THE BULLETIN BOARD OF FAITH

## THE RIGHT WORDS

*"Do not let your hearts be troubled. Trust in God; trust also in me. In my Father's house are many rooms. . . . I am going there to prepare a place for you."*

JOHN 14:2

## SPOKEN AT THE RIGHT TIME

Those who do not believe are often overwhelmed with the sorrows of this present time, but believers don't have to be overwhelmed. As followers of Christ, because we can trust in God, we, more than others, should keep our minds quiet when everything around us is noisy. His Word is truth. If He tells us that He has prepared a place for us in heaven, He has done just that.

## BRING UNDERSTANDING AND PEACE

I admit that I am not very creative when it comes to making bulletin board displays. I usually leave it up to the students—they are so much better at it than I am. But I always have one board devoted to showcasing the students' work. I call it our "brag board."

Every child does something worthy of praise, and I want to focus on what they have done right. I want them to be reminded of their successes when they walk into my room. In my mind's eye I can still see some of the work displayed. I see Charlie's book report on *Willy Wonka and the Chocolate Factory*. It was the first time he had ever completed an assignment. I knew he read the book because he and the main character had the same name. I kept that paper up all year. I wanted to remind him daily that he was indeed capable.

Then there was Sarah's theme on important people in her life. She wrote so eloquently about how her mother was the most important person in her life. Her mother had died earlier in the school year, and it touched me to see Sarah's heart revealed on paper for everyone to see. It was a brave thing to do, and she did it beautifully.

I read an incredible book by James Bryan Smith called *Room of Marvels* (Nashville: Broadman & Holman Publishers, 2004) that describes the room Christ has prepared for us in heaven. Covering the walls are pictures of people we've touched in our lives. It is a sort of testimony wall of our faith and love for God. As teachers I think we might have a bulletin board of faith waiting for us in our room.

This bulletin board is covered with the papers of the children we have touched throughout our careers, whether long or short. There are children and families you have touched that you may not even know about. There are colleagues who are different because of you. There are people who eventually came to a saving knowledge of Christ because of a small kindness you extended. I like to think each time we step outside ourselves and extend grace or choose to love or care for someone, no matter how briefly, more papers are stapled to that bulletin board in heaven. The best part is that God has arranged the bulletin board, so it is the most creative and attractive in the universe—and it displays *your* works of love and kindness.

ONE HEART AT A TIME

Live each day aware of the bulletin board of faith that is
being carefully created until you see it one day
in your room of marvels in heaven.

## PRAYER

*Lord, my mind is swimming with issues that bring me pain and discontentedness. I'm having trouble focusing on my life with you while my life here on earth is so noisy. Quiet my mind so that I can meditate on what is still to come.*

# 43

# RAISE YOUR HAND

## THE RIGHT WORDS

*Then I heard the voice of the Lord saying, "Whom shall I send?*
*Who will go for us?" "Here I am," I said; "send me!"*

ISAIAH 6:8 NAB

## SPOKEN AT THE RIGHT TIME

B elieving you have a divine appointment is powerful.
Sometimes we believe with great enthusiasm, and other
times we believe with fear and trembling. As those whom
God sends, we can be comforted that we go for God and
may therefore speak in His name. Since it is God who sends
us, we can be assured that He will bear us out.

## BRING UNDERSTANDING AND PEACE

L et me introduce you to a sweet spirit whose answer to God's call has inspired me to raise my hand in answer to God's call. Becky Clark is a teacher too! The following is her story.

Judy Garland sang in the 1948 musical *Easter Parade*, "I'm just a farm girl from Michigan." That's me. An eccentric farm girl.

I grew up talking to myself on my bike. I chatted to chickens while milking the cows. I preached eloquent, sad sermons for our departed kittens' funerals. Squirting milk at my cat's waiting whiskers—some into the milk pail—I even talked to God in the barn: *I don't know if you can ever use me, but I'd really like to be a teacher when I grow up.* My sister and I played school often, but I best liked teaching my twenty-five imaginary students perched up in Grandpa's pear tree.

Like David in the fields, God knew me, but nobody else did.

At twelve, I taped to my pink bedroom wall Isaiah 6:8: "Then I heard the voice of the Lord saying, 'Whom shall I send? Who will go for us?' 'Here I am,' I said; 'send me!'" I tried to talk my pastor into a missions trip to inner city Detroit, but for some reason he thought twelve was a little young to tackle gangs.

Everything about my first missions trip at seventeen impacted me. Our director challenged us to pray every day of the trip, "God, are you calling me into full-time missions?" I tried praying it. And an overwhelming burden for missions stunned me. I came home so fired up I made my sister go out in the cow pasture and preach with me. (I was imagining masses of lost souls.) I let her preach some, too, and I tried my hand at interpreting in Spanish. God bless our curious cows. They all crowded round as the most attentive congregation I've had to date.

I attended Bible college for missions and university for a teaching degree. I then taught in Africa at a missionary kid's school for three years. That overactive imagination came in handy, as I named my wretched cement housing "Rose Cottage." It got me through the rats in the kitchen, frogs in the toilet, and spiders in the shower.

In Africa, I learned some real life lessons about living for God, doing the right thing, and standing firm against the enemy's attacks. And I learned a whole lot from courageous, eccentric, ordinary vessels called missionaries.

I'm living in Asia now, homeschooling for one family. I'm only teaching one girl, not saving the lost *en masse*. I'm obeying God's call, yet I still feel like a kid in missions. I think it's how God keeps my face upturned to his. I don't know what country I'll move to next. I don't know if I'll ever be married—though I long for it. I am holding to my dreams, but most of all, I'm learning to trust God one day at a time.

# ONE HEART AT A TIME

Let your heart meditate on the refrain from the beautiful hymn "Here I Am, Lord" by Daniel L. Schutte.[1]

Here I am, Lord.
Is it I, Lord?
I have heard you calling in the night.
I will go, Lord,
If you lead me.
I will hold your people in my heart.

We are each called personally for His purposes and His delight. Stand tall, raise your hand, and say, "Here I am, Lord!"

## PRAYER

*Here I am, Lord, your servant. I know without a doubt that you have sent out a call for those who might teach your children. I will go. Send me. I have signed on the dotted line not knowing the cost. But I do know that no matter the cost you will be there to hold me up.*

# 44
# ℒIVING A LIFE WORTHY

## THE RIGHT WORDS

*And we pray this in order that you may live a life worthy of the Lord and may please him in every way; bearing fruit in every good work, growing in the knowledge of God, being strengthened with all power according to his glorious might so that you may have great endurance and patience, and joyfully giving thanks to the Father, who has qualified you to share in the inheritance of the saints in the kingdom of light.*

COLOSSIANS 1:10–12

## SPOKEN AT THE RIGHT TIME

The grace of God in the hearts of believers is the power of God, and there is glory in this power. Christians can draw on this strength in times of suffering. When we are weak, then we are strong, as God's grace is poured out in and through us. There is work to be done even when we are suffering. In all our trials we can give thanks to the Father of our Lord Jesus, whose grace has already equipped us to do the work ahead. We are also partakers of the inheritance provided for the saints.

## BRING UNDERSTANDING AND PEACE

It's so easy to get distracted by our human definition of *worthiness* and completely forget that it is God we are trying to please in our day-to-day life as a teacher of His children.

Between teacher evaluations, state testing mandates, the grading of schools, and state and federal expectations, our worthiness is always in question. I know that my frustration quite often rises in protest as a result.

We can use our jobs as teachers in worship to our heavenly Father. Each day in every way we can aspire to please Him. I admit that there are days when we don't feel qualified to do the work set before us. I also know that it is even more difficult to experience joy in the midst of substandard facilities, overly expectant parents, and less than stellar students. And yet we are qualified and we can have joy.

My greatest concern every day need not be "Will I be able to handle all that is thrust at me today?" Rather, I must focus on "Lord, help me to live this day worthy of your name." Everything else will either fall into place or disappear by its insignificance.

## ONE HEART AT A TIME

God's praise is all we really need and all we really want. He has equipped us for the work of our hands. He has qualified us as *worthy* through His Son. We can have joy in knowing these truths, no matter our circumstances. Circumstances change, but God's faithfulness never wavers.

### PRAYER

*Lamb of God, you are the Holy One, you are the Lord, and you alone are worthy. Now that I belong to you I know that I have been proclaimed worthy in your name and not my own. Help me to walk each and every day in a way worthy of your gift of grace.*

# 45

# ᏢUT ONE FOOT IN FRONT OF THE OTHER

## THE RIGHT WORDS

*Not only so, but we also rejoice in our sufferings, because we know that suffering produces perseverance; perseverance, character; and character, hope. And hope does not disappoint us, because God has poured out his love into our hearts by the Holy Spirit, whom he has given us.*

ROMANS 5:3–5

## SPOKEN AT THE RIGHT TIME

We stand firm and safe, no matter what the Enemy might do to us. Those of us who have hope in the glory of God have enough to rejoice in right now, no matter the circumstances. Tribulation works patience as the powerful grace of God works in and with it. Those who suffer patiently receive the outpouring of God's comfort. The more we suffer, the more grace abounds!

So when the day dawns and you know before even getting out of bed that it will not be a good day, rejoice! God's grace will abound, and we can wait in joyful hope of its coming.

## BRING UNDERSTANDING AND PEACE

My mother always told us that when things get tough to just put one foot in front of the other and walk. They were steps of hope. They were steps you took even when it all looked dark or disappointing.

There have been days when I awoke in the morning and cringed at the prospect of getting out of bed, let alone going to school. There have been times when I was so tired or so discouraged that I couldn't see the point of teaching one more day. Yet my mother's words rang through my ears—*Put one foot in front of the other!*

What is the alternative? The alternative is giving up, giving in, or walking out. I stopped looking through rose-colored glasses early in my teaching career. Every day in the classroom after that was a choice—a choice to go on teaching, to be joyful, to persevere.

There is something about suffering that polishes off our rough edges and makes us more attractive and pleasing to be around. It's the result of hope within us that makes others want to be around us, hoping to soak in whatever it is we're exuding. The confidence of a veteran teacher isn't the result of an easy ride. It's the result of persevering through difficult times and disappointing school years.

## ONE HEART AT A TIME

If you find yourself beginning to face terrific trials in teaching, don't despair! God is cultivating hope in you—hope that will carry you through the next trial and the next. It is a path *through* suffering that does this, not *around* it.

## PRAYER

*Lord, open the eyes of my heart so that I can see the hope this trial works in me. If I can't see a solution to the problem, let me rejoice in knowing that you are solving my problem by meeting my weakness with your strength.*

Worthy is as worthy does. We are not worthy on our own, we are only worthy because Christ took the blame and made us worthy through His death and resurrection. But as those proclaimed worthy, we must walk as worthy ones.

Our students aren't always worthy of our praise. In fact, they probably disappoint us more than they make us proud. There are students in your classroom today who struggle to walk worthy of the class they are in, the program they've qualified for, or your kindness. Can we show them what it means to walk worthy by our own walk?

They will learn perseverance first by our example and second by our encouragement. Christ showed us exactly how to live. He did not want us to be ignorant of it. As teachers we should not want our students to be ignorant of how to walk in the right way.

Which of your students struggles with perseverance? Can you commit to teaching them what it means to persevere and what perseverance looks like in your classroom? Pray for your strugglers today.

INTO YOUR HANDS, LORD . . .

*Pray for*

_____

_____

_____

_____

_____

*My flesh and my heart may fail, but God is the*
*strength of my heart and my portion forever.*
PSALM 73:26

# 46

# *G*REAT IS *Y*OUR
## FAITHFULNESS

## THE RIGHT WORDS

*Great is the Lord and most worthy of praise; his greatness no one*
*can fathom. One generation will commend your works to another;*
*they will tell of your mighty acts. They will speak of the glorious*
*splendor of your majesty; and I will meditate on your wonderful*
*works. They will tell of the power of your awesome works,*
*and I will proclaim your great deeds.*

PSALM 145:3–6

## SPOKEN AT THE RIGHT TIME

How do we know that God is good? We know by His
deeds. And those deeds are worthy of our praise even
when our own world seems to be falling apart. Often we
don't see how God was working in our lives until days,

months, even years later. God's faithfulness should not only be noted but shouted from the rooftops!

We have all experienced God's faithfulness and his greatness. We can and should speak of his wonderful works and pass down through the generations God's great deeds.

## BRING UNDERSTANDING AND PEACE

I have learned that God is good even when I seem to be the only one doing bus duty. God is good even when a student's parent calls me at 11:00 P.M. God is good even when I lose control of the class (and it isn't the first time). I learned this from various veteran teachers who were believers. It wasn't only their expertise I depended on; it was their faith.

I learned how to rest under the shelter of God's wings when a storm raged all around me in the teacher's lounge. I learned not to become irate when the district changed the language arts curriculum just when I was getting the hang of it. I learned to trust God with the fate of my students when there was nothing else I could do about a situation. I learned these things because men and women of faith taught them to me during break, during lunch, and during hall duty while we stood together. They weren't planned lessons, but inevitably there would be a test.

## ONE HEART AT A TIME

As you become a veteran teacher, ask God to reveal
opportunities for you to teach the younger, less
experienced teacher. I doubt you'll only be teaching
learning strategies—there will be faith strategies as well.

## PRAYER

*Lord, your works in my life and the lives of my
students are worthy of praise. Enable me to speak with
enthusiasm and clarity about your awesome deeds to those
who know you and those who don't know you yet. It does
my heart good to remember your good deeds in my life. It
increases my faith!*

# 47
# MILESTONE MARKERS

## THE RIGHT WORDS

*Abram traveled through the land as far as the site of the great tree
of Moreh at Shechem. . . . So he built an altar there to the Lord,
who had appeared to him. From there he (Abram) went on toward
the hills east of Bethel and pitched his tent, with Bethel on the
west and Ai on the east. There he built an altar to the Lord and
called on the name of the Lord. . . . So Abram moved his tents and
went to live near the great trees of Mamre at Hebron,
where he built an altar to the Lord.*

GENESIS 12:6–8; 13:18

## SPOKEN AT THE RIGHT TIME

As soon as Abram got to Canaan, he set up, and kept up,
the worship of God in his family. He not only kept the
ceremonial aspects of worship and the offering of sacrifice, but
he made a conscious effort to seek his God, calling on His

name; a spiritual sacrifice with which God is well pleased.

Abram was rich, had a large household, was unsettled, and living in the midst of enemies; yet wherever he pitched his tent, he built an altar. Wherever we go, let us not fail to take our faith along with us. Whether we teach in a public or private school, we need to take the time to offer spiritual sacrifice to our God.

## BRING UNDERSTANDING AND PEACE

Over the course of my teaching career I have had six classrooms. Each time I moved, I organized my room following the same ritual. I always liked my desk set up a certain way. I always hung an "About Me" bulletin board behind my desk. I always had two bookcases—one filled with books on teaching and the other with my favorite fiction. My desk always had stand-up files and mementoes to remind me of the kindnesses of previous students and parents. Finally, I would place my Bible on the lower left corner of my desk along with a perpetual verse-a-day calendar.

The Bible was the last thing I set out. It completed the room. It was the finishing touch. But it wasn't the end of the story.

Having the Bible within reach and view did help me to be more faithful with a quiet time before students arrived each day. More important, it reminded me that I was where I was because God brought me there.

It's so easy to get bogged down in the busyness of the teaching day. It's so easy to forget why I am where I am and who put me there. I needed a physical reminder—an altar of sorts—to help me remember these important truths. And when I was having trouble with a student or was preparing for a difficult parent conference, one look at my Bible reminded me again of who was in control—and it certainly wasn't me!

## ONE HEART AT A TIME

We can mark our comings and goings with a tangible sign.
We can create something to touch, to look at to help us
meditate on the faithfulness of the God who directs our
steps and marks out our paths. The well-worn leather
cover of my first King James Bible was and
continues to be my mile marker.

## PRAYER

*Lord, God, you are the path that I follow, the pursuit of my life. You alone are responsible for the blessings I experience. Help me to be mindful of how you direct my steps. I will take the time now to meditate on your faithfulness.*

# 48
## ℐHE KING IS ON HIS THRONE

### THE RIGHT WORDS

*The Lord sits enthroned over the flood; the Lord is enthroned as King forever. The Lord gives strength to his people; the Lord blesses his people with peace.*

PSALM 29:10–11

### SPOKEN AT THE RIGHT TIME

God wasn't an absent ruler when the flood waters covered the earth. During the most horrific disaster in history, God was on His throne. He strengthened Noah and his family and then blessed them for their obedience.

The trials that trouble our minds and bodies are not outside of God's view or His will. God gives us strength and purpose and will bless us in our perseverance and faith.

## BRING UNDERSTANDING AND PEACE

H as your school day, or school year for that matter, ever felt as if you were in the middle of a deadly tornado? The needs of students and demands of administration swirl around you like debris that will tear you to shreds if it touches you in the whirlwind. God is on His throne!

Have you ever had some personal crisis that seemed like a blood-thirsty wolf you couldn't keep at bay, threatening to consume you? Do you battle with a chronic illness or chronic mental or spiritual struggle that clouds your judgment and thwarts your plans of being a good teacher? God is on His throne!

The year I went back to work and had to put my younger child in day care was the most overwhelming, disappointing, and frustrating year of my career. Daily disasters plagued me. Frequent failures nipped at my heels. I was drowning, slowly but surely.

And yet God was on His throne!

God isn't a king who sits and ignores the cries of His people. He is above—but not above our pain and pleas. He is in control—all sovereign, all powerful, all knowing—and He's all mine! I knew intellectually that this was true. And in the midst of my trial, He upheld me. I didn't drown. I was not destroyed.

## ONE HEART AT A TIME

Each time you face a potentially overwhelming trial, you
can stop, right in the middle of it, and rest—rest in
the knowledge, proven to you personally, that
God our King is indeed on His throne.

## PRAYER

*Praise and honor and glory are yours! Lord, God, you
alone are the Holy One, you alone are the Lord, you alone
are the Most High. I lift my face to you even while
everything around me is falling apart. Uphold me with
your right hand and grant me your blessing!*

# 49

# GENTLEMEN AND GENTLEWOMEN

## THE RIGHT WORDS

*But the fruit of the Spirit is love, joy, peace, patience, kindness, goodness, faithfulness, gentleness and self-control. Against such things there is no law. Those who belong to Christ Jesus have crucified the sinful nature with its passions and desires. Since we live by the Spirit, let us keep in step with the Spirit.*

GALATIANS 5:22–25

## SPOKEN AT THE RIGHT TIME

Paul names the fruit of the Spirit, which tends to make Christians agreeable to one another as well as makes them happy. The fruit of the Spirit evidences that we are led by the Spirit.

Those of us who walk the halls of a public school can

boldly live by the Spirit and exhibit this fruit without fear that we have broken some law. We can live out our faith, get along with others, and be happy all at the same time.

## BRING UNDERSTANDING AND PEACE

D o you remember the television series *Gentle Ben*? It was about a boy who befriended an orphaned black bear cub in the Florida Everglades. When I think of the attribute of gentleness, I think of Gentle Ben.

We never questioned the bear's strength or his ability to tear a man apart if he wanted to. We knew that even though he was tamed, he was still a wild animal. Gentleness is tempered with strength, ability, and power. Gentleness is not the equivalent of a pushover. The bear's wild side had been harnessed and turned to serve the boy who loved him.

Do you have a wild side as a teacher? I know that in the beginning of my career I lost my temper more often than I kept it. I knew I had power over my students and that their future was in my hands. That's an awesome responsibility, and sometimes that power is abused.

As teachers who are capable, we can be strict yet fair; have high expectations yet show compassion; we can be stern yet be under control. Our power and might needs to be harnessed and bent to serve the will of God.

Gentle men and gentle women we can be!

## ONE HEART AT A TIME

It is good to know what the fruit of the Spirit is as well as
what the works of the flesh are so that we can nurture and
cultivate the fruit of the Spirit in ourselves and
avoid and oppose the works of the flesh.

## PRAYER

*My heavenly Father, you are the best teacher. Your
Spirit shows me what it means to follow you. Day by day
renew my inner being so that ultimately I will look,
sound, and act like you.*

# 50

# *O*PEN CLASSROOM,
# OPEN HEART

## THE RIGHT WORDS

*Then Jesus said to his host, "When you give a luncheon or dinner,*
*do not invite your friends, your brothers or relatives, or your rich*
*neighbors; if you do, they may invite you back and so you will be*
*repaid. But when you give a banquet, invite the poor, the crippled,*
*the lame, the blind, and you will be blessed. Although they cannot*
*repay you, you will be repaid at the resurrection of the righteous."*

LUKE 14:12–14

## SPOKEN AT THE RIGHT TIME

So often we tend to do things for others in the secret hope
of being repaid someday. "Think of all I did for him!"
you may hear yourself say. Or you may hear others say, "What
he's done to me is like a slap in the face!" But our motivation

to serve or minister to others should be from a heart of love and compassion. We will be repaid someday—on the last day. It's the day we live for.

## BRING UNDERSTANDING AND PEACE

I always had an *open classroom* policy. I wanted parents to feel comfortable coming in to visit whenever it was convenient for *them*. Staying open carried a certain risk. I never knew who might enter.

And then Mrs. Williams came to visit.

Mary Williams was the homeschooling mom of five children. She was thinking about putting her oldest son back into public school—specifically into my class. She and Shane visited our class every day for two weeks. They said nothing. They did nothing. They just stayed for an hour or so and then smiled at me politely when they left. As much as I wanted to be *open* to them, I was terrified, wondering what they thought of my teaching and our class.

Later I discovered that the Williams family had visited two other fifth-grade classrooms, but with less frequency than they visited mine. Ultimately, Mrs. Williams decided against putting Shane back into public school. I was afraid it was because of something she saw in my class.

My principal called me into his office and handed me a letter. It was from Mrs. Williams.

"I decided that Shane is not ready to go back into [public] school. I saw, much to my delight, what an energetic, creative classroom looked like when we visited you. When and if we decide to send Shane or any of our other children back to school, we'll look for a teacher and a classroom like yours. Thank you for allowing us to invade your space."

Her letter not only brought relief, but a humble sense of being used for purposes not my own.

## ONE HEART AT A TIME

An open-door policy at your school should have little to do with the school's image and everything to do with God's reputation. An open heart opens doors without being asked and without expecting a favor in return.

## PRAYER

*Lord, you gave your only begotten Son so that the gates of heaven would be flung open for me. You did it without thought of repayment, knowing that I could never repay you. You did it out of sacrificial love to reconcile me to yourself. If I can offer even a tiny taste of your mercy to my students, I am grateful for the chance.*

We've spent this book focusing our prayers on those around us—whether colleagues, students, or parents. There are definite needs to pray for during the school year. But now it's time to focus on your own needs and bring them before the Lord. God can change your heart no matter how impossible it may seem. You may have habits, attitudes, or choices for which you need prayer. There may be changes coming in your school that concern you. There may be children whose future is uncertain. Prayer can lead to peace for yourself and others if you allow God to work in your heart and mold you into His image. Sometimes this can be a painful process, but the result is glorifying and glorious!

Open yourself to God now. Ask Him to search your heart and reveal to you any concern—past, present, or future—that you should bring to Him. With prayer and obedience God can bring you peace.

### INTO YOUR HANDS, LORD . . .

*Pray for*

_____

_____

*Let the words of my mouth, and the meditation of my heart, be acceptable in thy sight, O Lord, my strength, and my redeemer.*
PSALM 19:14 KJV

# *Endnotes*

## Chapter 1

1. *Matthew Henry's Complete Commentary on the Whole Bible* (Peabody, Mass: Hendrickson Publishers, 1991).

## Chapter 21

1. *Matthew Henry's Concise Commentary on the Whole Bible,* *http://bible.crosswalk.com/Commentaries/Matthew-HenryConcise/mhc-con.cgi?book=2co&chapter=009.*

## Chapter 24

1. *Matthew Henry's Concise Commentary on the Whole Bible,* *http://bible.crosswalk.com/Commentaries/Matthew-HenryConcise/mhc-con.cgi?book=1pe&chapter=005.*

## Chapter 37

1. "Jesus, Name Above All Names" © 1974 Scripture in Song (% Integrity Music) ASCAP % Integrity Media, Inc., 1000 Cody Road, Mobile, AL 36695.

## Chapter 43

1. "Here I am Lord" by Daniel Schutte © 1981, OCP Publications, 5536 NE Hassalo, Portland, Oregon 97213. All rights reserved. Used with permission.